engraved by grace

Esther Burroughs

Engraved by Grace

Books by Esther Burroughs
available from New Hope Publishers

Treasures of a Grandmother's Heart

Empowered

A Garden Path to Mentoring

Engraved by Grace

CREATING A LEGACY *of* FAITH
for YOUR CHILDREN

Esther Burroughs

new
hope
PUBLISHERS

Birmingham, Alabama

New Hope® Publishers
P. O. Box 12065
Birmingham, AL 35202-2065
www.newhopepublishers.com

© 2005 by Esther Burroughs
All rights reserved. First printing 2005
Printed in the United States of America

No part of this publication may be reproduced, stored in a retrieval system, or transmitted in any form or by any means—electronic, mechanical, photocopying, recording, or otherwise—without the prior written permission of the publisher.

Library of Congress Cataloging-in-Publication Data

Burroughs, Esther.
  Engraved by grace : creating a legacy of faith for your children / by Esther Burroughs.
     p. cm.
  ISBN 1-56309-987-X (hardcover)
  1. Christian education--Home training. I. Title.
  BV1590.B87 2005
  248.8'45--dc22

                                   2005018342

All scripture quotations, unless otherwise indicated, are taken from the New King James Version. Copyright © 1982 by Thomas Nelson, Inc. Used by permission. All rights reserved.

Scripture quotations marked (NASB) are taken from the New American Standard Bible®, Copyright © 1960, 1962, 1963, 1968, 1971, 1972, 1973, 1975, 1977, 1995 by The Lockman Foundation. Used by permission.

Scripture quotations marked (NIV) are taken from the HOLY BIBLE, NEW INTERNATIONAL VERSION®. NIV®. Copyright©1973, 1978, 1984 by International Bible Society. Used by permission of Zondervan. All rights reserved.

Scripture quotations marked (AMP) are taken from the Amplified® Bible, Copyright © 1954, 1958, 1962, 1964, 1965, 1987 by The Lockman Foundation. Used by permission.

Scripture quotations marked (TLB) are taken from *The Living Bible*, copyright© 1971. Used by permission of Tyndale House Publishers, Inc., Wheaton, IL. All rights reserved.

Scripture quotations marked (NRSV) are taken from the New Revised Standard Version Bible, copyright 1989, by the Division of Christian Education of the National Council of the Churches of Christ in the U.S.A. Used by permission. All rights reserved.

Scripture quotations marked (*The Message*) are taken from *The Message* by Eugene H. Peterson. Copyright © 1993, 1994, 1995, 1996, 2000, 2001, 2002. Used by permission of NavPress Publishing Group."

ISBN: 1-56309-987-X
N054127 • 0106 • 2M2

*T*o the memory of my mother,
Neva Dell Milligan,
whose faith journey became my legacy.

To my sister, Moyra Milligan Munroe, whose
grace journey is becoming my legacy.
She cared for my mother in those hard
days as she died of Alzheimer's. I struggled
not being close to help with Mother's care,
until my sister *engraved grace* upon
my heart with these words:

> *God called me to care for Mother,*
> *and He called you to speak. Now*
> *you do your job and I'll do mine.*

I give honor to these two
remarkable women in my life.

I wish to also thank these faithful friends
whom I asked to pray for me and encourage
me during the writing of this book:

Chris Adams	*Kitty Herndon*
Rebekah Babb	*Jody Hoffman*
Henry Blackaby	*Dr. Jack & Millie Humphries*
Eva Gay Brown	*Susan Lafferty*
Becky & Ray Brown	*Tara Miller*
Deborah Burnett	*David/Pat Milligan*
Leslie Caldwell	*Debbie Moss*
Barbara Curnutt	*Beth Perkins*
Dr. Leisa DeVenny	*Lanara Southard*
Rebecca England	*Scott Terry*
Cindy Gaskins	*Sheila West*
Virginia Greene	*Karla Worley*

contents

After my high school graduation in the summer of 1955, I packed my trunk in preparation for college, which was thousands of miles from home. I was leaving my home on the west coast of Canada, and I knew I would not be coming home until I completed my degree at Mars Hill College in North Carolina. My parents simply could not afford for me to travel back home for holidays and summer. I would be working each summer to pay the next semester's bills.

With the hope of a college degree in front of me and the certainty that Mars Hill was where God wanted me to be, I packed all my worldly possessions into a small army trunk. Tucked between my clothes was the hope of a young Canadian woman, surrendered to follow God's call, not certain what that might look like, not dreaming where God would lead, just certain that God *would* lead. Leaving Edmonton, Alberta, Canada, I said a tearful goodbye to my mother as she handed me a sack lunch. The bus trip took four days and three nights. The lunch lasted two!

As my father said goodbye to me, he said he wanted to give me a "jewel." I did not own one piece of jewelry, so my mind raced ahead, thinking he might be giving me a ring! He quietly announced that the "jewel" he had for me would become more precious to me each year I was away from home. Little did I know how right he was! His gift to me was Proverbs 3:5–6:

> *"Trust in the LORD with all your heart, and lean not on your own understanding; in all your ways acknowledge Him, and He shall direct your paths."*

That jewel became a legacy on my faith journey…
> engraved on my mind
> underlined in my Bible
> embroidered on my heart.

What transpired that day was the passing of a *baton of faith* from one generation to another. How it sustained me! How it carried me in my heart! How it assured me! From that day on, I felt like my father was speaking that Scripture truth to me every time I read it. Certainly my heavenly Father was standing over me, teaching me to trust in Him for everything. Proverbs 3:5–6 is etched in my very fiber of my being, and I'm determined to pass the baton of God's promises to the generations yet to be born.

My challenge to my readers is, whether you be a parent, godparent, aunt, uncle, grandparent, or spiritual parent, you have a tremendous privilege and command from God's Word to make a difference by passing the baton of faith to the next generation, imprinting God's love on the next generation. Not everyone receives an inheritance from parents or grandparents. But everyone leaves a legacy. It is the life you live, your experiences, in family and community. God's Word commands us to tell His story to the next generation, even to those yet to be born. We must tell God's story to *this* generation, trusting God that our faithfulness will be passed on to the generations to come. Read aloud the words of Psalm 78:5–7 (NASB):

> *"For He established a testimony in Jacob and appointed a law in Israel, which He commanded our fathers that they should teach them to their children, that the generation to come might know, even the children yet to be born* [that's my great-grandchildren], *that they may arise and tell them to their children, that they should put their confidence in God and not forget the works of God, but keep His commandments…"*

And in the next breath, the psalmist cautions:

> *"…and not be like their fathers, a stubborn and rebellious generation, a generation that did not prepare its heart and whose spirit was not faithful to God."*

My heart fears that even in Christian homes, children are not learning God's love, truth, and grace as an integral part of family life. We must become runners in the race of life and intentionally pass on the baton of faith to our children, grandchildren, friends, and community, and to generations to come. God commands it. May this generation be found faithful in obedience and not stubborn like our spiritual forefathers.

In Isaiah 49:16, God tells us: *"See, I have engraved you on the palms of my hands"* (NIV). His signature is forever engraved on our hearts. The people of Zion had been lamenting that God has forgotten them, and the Lord answered:

> *"Can a woman forget her nursing child, that she should not have compassion on the son of her womb? Yes, they may forget, yet I will not forget you.* [What a promise!] *Behold, I have indelibly imprinted you on the palm of each of My hands; your walls are continually before Me."*
> —Isaiah 49:15–16 (AMP)

God will remember His people. Our heavenly Father has indelibly imprinted your name on the palm of both of His hands. Precious friend, that's grace…you have been *engraved by grace.*

Consider the cost He paid for you to be engraved with His love. May you be challenged to pass the baton of faith to this generation and the generations yet to be born. Whatever you do, don't drop the baton!

EB

"This will be written for the generation to come, that a people yet to be created may praise the LORD."

—Psalm 102:18

Legacies of Faith

As I was driving our grandtwins to my home from playschool one day, our grandson, Walker, who was age four at that time, said, "God's bigger than anything, isn't He, Nana?" Before I could answer, he continued. "He's all over the place. Right, Nana?" "That's right, Walker!" I responded. Walker pursued the subject. "Even all the time, even when you can't see Him, He is still bigger than anything. Right, Nana? Yup, He's bigger than anything in the whole world," he concluded.

Oh, for the faith of a child! I call these moments "God Stops." God Stops are moments when God's love bursts through in a family, and they are bound closer to God and to each other. God is the one who creates these moments, but we can prepare the way for the Lord by the way we live in front of our children, by the way we order our families' lives around the teachings of Jesus, and by the daily reminders of God's truth that we place in our children's paths.

I believe you and I should be living in such bold faith that our children literally beg us to teach them how to trust in God in life's circumstances. They should be seeing us praying. They should be seeing us exercising our trust in God. They should experience our faith working and that should inspire them to want to live like that.

As I write these words, I have several family situations that make me feel as if I'm crossing the Mississippi in an inner tube, and I'm faith-ing that the God of Israel will indeed part the waters for me and my family. He is the God of miracles, and I'm really looking for one! I am His daughter, and He is looking for me to be found faithful in believing. I want my children to feel my faith as I walk in and with Christ.

Faithful—from Generation to Generation

The study of God's Word proves my grandson's theology correct. In the Old Testament, we can all see the hand of God that stretches from generation to generation, never veering from His plan of redemption and intimacy with His children. He *is* bigger than everything. From beginning to end…He *is* everything. I want to believe like a child.

When I was growing up, I was constantly reminded by my parents to turn off the lights. After all, it *did* cost money. I still automatically turn off the lights when I leave a room—because that message was ingrained in me by repetition. Children still learn by repetition. But never once are we scolded by God about turning off any lights. Rather, we are told repeatedly by our heavenly Father to *walk in the light*. The lamp of God is eternal and still dispelling the darkness today.

God is Light! In the beginning, God pronounced: "*Let there be light!*" (Genesis 1:3). He announces His Son's birth with the light of a star and closes His Book with the star still shining.

> God spoke: *Let there be light…*
> …and there was.
> God placed His star in the east…
> …and there He is.
> Jesus speaks: *I am the Light…*
> …and He always will be.
> Jesus commands: *Let your light shine…*
> …but will we?

In Revelation 22:16, Jesus speaks about His light, saying, "*I, Jesus, have sent My angel to testify to you these things in the churches. I am the Root and Offspring of David, the Bright and Morning Star.*" He then reminds us, "*I am coming quickly."* The lamp of God is the Alpha and the Omega, the beginning and the end. He is trusting you and me to be His light to another generation.

Joshua Carried the Light

Remember the story of Joshua leading the children of Israel into the Promised Land? It's in the Bible Book of Joshua, chapters 3 and 4. Moses had died, and Joshua had the awesome task of taking Israel into Canaan. The Lord told him to cross the Jordan River, taking the Ark of the Covenant in front. He must have been afraid, for sure, to do this assignment! But as the priests carrying the ark touched the river, the waters dried up and they crossed on dry land. (You may recall this is not the first time God's mighty hand dried up the waters for His people! See Exodus 14.) Now that's a *God Stop*, if there ever was one!

When they had crossed, God told Joshua: *"Take up for yourselves twelve stones from here out of the middle of the Jordan, from the place where the priests' feet are standing firm, and carry them over with you and lay them down in the lodging place where you will lodge tonight"* (Joshua 4:3 NASB). Joshua followed the Lord's command, and told the people, *"Let this be a sign among you, so that when your children ask later, saying, 'What do these stones mean to you?' then you shall say to them, 'Because the waters of the Jordan were cut off before the ark of the covenant of the* LORD'" (Joshua 4:6–7 NASB).

This question begs for an answer. *What do these stones mean to you?* Notice it does not say, *What does this mean?* It does not say, *What does this mean to us?* It says, *What do these stones mean to you?*

I can hear one of the Israelite children asking, "Mama, what do the stones mean to you?" Mama answers, "These stones remind me that God showed us a miracle today. We built this altar to give thanks to God." In my mind, I'm thinking that the child might run to get his own stones to add to the altar! This is just what children do…they imitate adults!

Be on the lookout for those *teachable moments* with your children and teach them the ways of God. Listen carefully to their questions. They have much to teach us about God's ways.

When my first granddaughter, Anna Esther, was in preschool, she attended music time at her church one afternoon a week. One evening when she came home, she was really wired. Her mom, Melody, suggested they lay down on the bed for a little quiet time. Getting Anna to do so was not that easy, but Melody asked what she learned at church that day. Anna said, "Mommy, remember when Jesus feeds all the people and there is just gobs left

It was a sacred moment—not unlike when the Israelites built the memorial—and our hearts were engraved with this message: God did it!

over? That was the story." Melody asked her, "Well, how do you think that happened?" Getting close to her mother's face, Anna whispered, "*God did it.*"

It was a sacred moment—not unlike when the Israelites built the memorial—and our hearts were engraved with this message: God did it!

Faith in Front of Them

Shortly after the 9/11 tragedy, I was on the phone with Anna Esther, who was then a teenager. I was about to leave on a trip, and she asked, "Nana, are you still going to fly?" "Yes," I responded. "I knew it!" was her reply. Faith is the essence of my personal spiritual journey. On my first trip out after that terrible tragedy, don't think I didn't pray on that plane, *I believe, God help my unbelief.* It was a faith walk, before God—and before my first grandchild. It left a memory…for her and for me.

Let me encourage you who are parents of young children to look for those *God moments* with your children that give you teachable *faith-building* encounters. Look for every opportunity to impact their hearts with Godly truth.

I received an email sharing several thoughts an 8-year-old boy had said about God. This one is my favorite: "If you don't believe in God, besides being an atheist, you will be very lonely, because your parents can't go everywhere with you, like to camp, but God can." When you begin early in a child's life looking for, planning for, and enjoying *faith-building moments,* you are building an *altar of remembrance* to Holy God and walking in obedience to His commands. A lovely surprise awaits as you watch your children grow to become teenagers, then to grown adults, and watch them establish their own family worship traditions and rituals, engraving another generation of Godly homes, following God's commands.

Dr. Gary Ezzo is the author of the best-selling book *Growing Kids God's Way.* Some time back, I heard this story. I'll pass it along to you.

Early in their marriage, Gary and Ann Marie attended their church one evening and heard a missionary speak about her work in her mission field. In telling her mission experience, she invited the church body to give a love gift for the mission work. Deeply touched, Anne Marie punched Gary in the side (that's one of the tasks of a wife!) and whispered, "We have $17.25 in our checking account and I think we should write a check for $17.00." He shook his head, "No." The missionary continued to speak, further convicting Ann Marie, and once again, after asking Gary to write a check, he shook his head "No" a second time. The third time, when Anne Marie made her request, he whispered to Ann Marie, "Write a check for $17.25." She did! I wonder what it was like that week, with NO money in the bank account! About a week later, Gary picked up the mail and found an envelope from a job he had forgotten he had done. He opened the envelope and a check for $34.50 fell out. Get it? Double their gift to the missionary! You can't outgive God!

This is not the end of this story! Gary Ezzo now has the check framed, and it is hanging on the wall by his rocking chair in the family room. When his grandchildren rock in his lap, point to the check, and ask, "Papa, what does that mean to you?" Gary tells the story of God's faithfulness in their life. A *legacy* hangs on the wall of the Ezzo home—engraving the story on the hearts of children and grandchildren.

Isaiah 43:10 reminds us:

> *"You are my witness," says the LORD, "and My servant whom I have chosen, that you may know and believe Me, and understand that I am He. Before Me there was no God formed, nor shall there be after Me."*

Dear reader, every one of us is a *witness* and each one is a *servant* of the living God! As a servant of the living God, learn to tell your *God stories* over and over again—engraving them on the hearts of your children, grandchildren, and spiritual children—until it becomes part of their *faith-story memory bank*. Fill their memory bank full, so that in times of need your children can withdraw your faith stories and be encouraged by following your example. This is a huge task and responsibility. You must be intentional about passing on your *baton of faith*.

You can go to a Christian bookstore and look for age-appropriate educational devotional material. You will be delighted to see the wealth of resources to help families develop traditions and rituals.

In the introduction of her journal book, *Daily Light*, Anne Graham Lotz writes these words:

> *When I was a young girl growing up in my parent's home, we had family Bible reading and prayer every day. After breakfast, my mother would gather us in the kitchen and read a brief passage of Scripture. We would then slip down on our knees as she led us in seeking God's guidance and blessing for the day. My mother's faithfulness in leading her family into God's presence on a consistent, daily basis is a blessing I will carry with me all my life. By her example, she demonstrated her dependency on the Lord, her trust in His Word, and her steadfast desire to claim all He had for us. But growing up, my favorite times of Bible reading were led by my father. Since it was Mother's habit to lead us in the morning, when Daddy was home, he usually led us in the evening. Instead of hastily gathering us in the kitchen before dashing off to school, we operated on a more relaxed pace as we sat together in the living room. My father would read a passage of Scripture, pausing as he read to comment or explain what he was reading. Even as a young girl, my heart was quickened by his informal teaching, and I deeply desired to*

understand more about the Scripture than just a
surface reading afforded.

Morning and evening Bible reading and prayers—quite a
legacy for the five Graham children—all of whom serve in
some kind of ministry around the world!

Give praise to God, right now! You and I are *covenant
people*. God is the *Covenant Maker*. He has been faithful to
the Graham family and yours.

I was recently astounded once again in a Bible study
time at God's eternal compassion for His covenant with the
children of Israel and with us. Remember that David's son,
Solomon, followed him on the throne, and had his moment
in his generation to follow the Lord, but he dropped the
baton!

Read aloud 1 Kings 11:6–13 to see what I mean.

> *"Solomon did evil in the sight of the LORD, and
> did not fully follow the LORD, as did his father
> David. Then Solomon built a high place for
> Chemosh the abomination of Moab, on the hill
> that is east of Jerusalem, and for Molech the
> abomination of the people of Ammon. And he
> did likewise for all his foreign wives, who
> burned incense and sacrificed to their gods. So
> the LORD became angry with Solomon, because
> his heart had turned from the LORD God of
> Israel, who had appeared to him twice, and
> commanded him concerning this thing, that he*

should not go after other gods; but he did not keep what the LORD had commanded. Therefore the LORD said to Solomon, 'Because you have done this, and have not kept My covenant and My statutes, which I commanded you, I will surely tear the kingdom away from you and give it to your servant. Nevertheless I will not do it in your days, for the sake of your father David; I will tear it out of the hand of your son. However I will not tear away the whole kingdom; I will give one tribe to your son for the sake of My servant David, and for the sake of Jerusalem which I have chosen.'"

What a legacy of faithfulness King David left for generations coming behind him! It is such a legacy that God chose not to completely wipe out King Solomon's heritage—rather, saving it for one of his sons. This promise was all about King David's faithfulness to God and God's faithfulness to David. I'm stunned by these words. Related to my own personal faithfulness, my heart cries out with this question—*What would God choose to save for another generation, because of my faithfulness?*

This is certainly something about which to think. No! It is something to act upon *now*. Start your family traditions. Delay no longer. A godly heritage will last. May our legacies be a *lamp to God* to another generation.

As you read this book, may I suggest that you look up and mark every Scripture in this book in your own Bible?

The Bible is *God-breathed* and you do not want to miss hearing His Spirit speak to you.

Look at 1 Kings 11:36. The writer is explaining God's desire related to David's faithfulness: *"And to his son I will give one tribe, that My servant David may always have a lamp before Me in Jerusalem, the city which I have chosen for Myself, to put My name there."*

God keeps a light on in Jerusalem, the city where He chose to put His name.

What a legacy he left you and me. We are His temple, and He has put His name in us, through His Spirit, and left His light on, in you and me.

On October 14, 2004, at 8:10 AM, I was writing this chapter about the lamp of God promised to David's descendants when the lights flickered in my study room and then went out! Immediately, I got up and flicked the light switch off and on several times. A light went on in my head as I remembered the notice we had received earlier in the week from Alabama Power Company stating that our power would go out intermittently for the next week—for one or two minutes and up to four hours. I quit worrying about it and sat down to write on my battery-powered Mac iBook! Aren't you glad God isn't dependent on a power company for light? More than that, the *lamp of God* promised to David NEVER goes out...is never intermittent...is never dependent on anyone or anything! His light was set in eternity when He spoke light into being in Genesis 1:3.

Like the disobedient children of Israel, my light some-times flickers. My light is often intermittent. No wonder the world is confused with so many *flickering lights!* If another generation is to see His light in us, we must consider the God who put the light of Christ in us, and then instructs us not to put it under a bushel, but to let it shine. Remember the little chorus: *Don't let Satan blow it out. No! I'm gonna let it shine!* Have you noticed how easy it is to shine so brightly for Jesus on Sunday, and then on Monday, how easy it is for Satan to get to us through life with our family? Satan is the *Chief Wind Bag* when it comes to blowing out our candles.

Remember: a child of light...

relies on the Giver of light...

to become bearer of light!

Remembering Your Heritage

Just this past week, in October 2004, I received in the mail the grave stone markings of Bob's parents—the *Burroughs* —and my grandparents, the *Milligan* family. My grand-mother, Annie Hall McKee Milligan, is my father's mother. She lived to be 90 years of age! My father recently gave me a typed 3x5 note card—with the minister's notes about Grandmother—spoken by the preacher at her funeral. All these years later, these words call me to be faithful, as my grandmother was faithful:

*"There was a wonderful dignity about Grandma Milligan. She was not a social butterfly, but she was a true **mother of Israel**, a faithful member whose faith was full of Christ. Her going home gives a challenge to the family to be imitators of Grandma as she was an imitator of Christ, and a challenge for someone to rise up and fill the gap with the same integrity and Christian grace."*

Part of my *faith-building story* comes from time spent with my mother's mother, Mildred Esther Woods, in Drumheller, Alberta, Canada. As a child, I saw Grandmother on her screened porch, in her reading chair, with her Bible open, and often on her knees in prayer. I remember peeking in on her and feeling loved and safe. I loved Grandmother very much and remember her soft and tender spirit towards me.

When I was with her, she would always brush my hair ringlets, then put a bow in my hair, and always put an apron on me as she let me work with her in the kitchen. Guess what I do with my grandkids? I bake with them in the kitchen, of course, as we make messes, laugh, and make memories. Maybe I should have copied the apron idea! My heart trusts these moments to my grandchildren's memory bank and, hopefully, they will repeat the lessons with their children in years to come.

I loved the way my grandmother whistled and sang the hymns, as did my mother, not even aware she was doing it. I loved bedtime prayers and kisses from my grandmother. At times, I can still breathe in her fragrance, hear the crunch of her footsteps on the cinder sidewalk, and remember the wooden path to the outhouse—where the out-of-season Sears catalogue was placed, for obvious reasons. I am grateful she passed *the baton of faith* to my mother and that my mother passed it to me.

My mother once told me about the time my grandmother, who was a new Christian, had saved her money to buy a fur stole. She was so pleased with herself—until she learned that her church planned a sacrificial mission offering. Her heart melted. She never got the fur stole. Instead, she gave all the money to the mission project. I've seen my parents do the same kind of giving, and I've learned from them, and now I'm watching my children do the same. These are legacies of faith...well remembered.

Building Memorials

Ebenezer. Now, that is a difficult word to pronounce—and what on earth does it mean? I wondered this as a child when we sang the hymn "Come, Thou Fount of Every Blessing," which has these words, "Here I raise mine Ebenezer." Oh, you'll want to know this! Recall with me the story from 1 Samuel 7. It seems that Israel was often running from or into the Philistines. On one occasion, they asked the prophet, Samuel, to pray to God for protection. As the Philistines came close, God provided a huge thunderclap, exploding among the Philistines, who then turned and ran—with Israel in hot pursuit (1 Samuel 7:10). To honor God's provision, Samuel took a single rock and stood it up between Mizpah and Shen. He named the stone Ebenezer, literally, "stone of help," saying, "This marks the place where God helped us." (Read 1 Samuel 7:1–13).

I love verse 12, which says: *"Thus far the LORD has helped us."* Today, we might say, "So far, the Lord has helped us!" What a faith statement! As covenant children, don't forget to raise *your* stone of remembrance.

Several years ago, our daughter and her family were moving from Atlanta, Georgia, to Greenville, South Carolina. Knowing her concern, I suggested that my daughter and her husband pray with their daughters about the sale and purchase of their homes, and allow their girls to experience God's faithfulness in answered prayer. I remember being asked to pray for just the right location...the right price...the right church...the right school, and of course, the right work. I watched...and prayed...and watched... and prayed. God watched...and answered. *Ebenezer!* As of this writing in late 2004, they are praying together as a family about another move. Every family has had experiences where they can say, "So far the Lord has helped us." This would make a great family motto! Creating faith legacies is about building rituals and celebrations that will be copied and remembered. When family gets together, an oft-used phrase is, "Remember when we...." These moments are the glue that bonds families. Make memories.

In the 1970s, I served as the part-time campus minister at Samford University, in Birmingham, Alabama. One time,

I was preparing a group of 19 students to travel to New York City for a ministry project on the lower east side of Manhattan. We had the January term to study missions and make spiritual and physical preparations. It was a life-changing experience for this writer as well as for many of the students. As we gathered wood, paint, and work tools from the churches of the team members, we saw *God stop* after *God stop*. Our assignment was to renovate a bar, preparing it for an after-school care program. It was later to be named Graffiti. The team was chosen...the plans were made.

Several times during the month's preparation, the students met in our home to eat, get team assignments, and pray. I included my children as much as possible—at that time, David was in the fourth grade and Melody was in the seventh. One evening, without my knowledge, my son was sitting on the steps listening while we were praying for our needs. We had learned to pray very boldly for specific needs. The next morning, my son appeared in the kitchen and said to me, "Mom, I heard the team praying last night and I want to help with this mission and give them all my allowance savings, for gas money." It was $8.32! I was amazed. He continued: "I want you to give it to the team and you tell them I will pray that when they fill up the van, the gas will last a long time. Is that okay Mom?"

Thus far the Lord has helped us. Our son David had seen the baton of faith in his grandparents and parents, and was learning to pass it along. You will not be surprised to know that today David leads a mission organization called

PASSPORT, which is touching the lives of teenagers who minister around the world! The legacy lived in your home will teach your children to keep passing the baton of faith to generations yet to be born.

David's children—our grandtwins Milligan and Walker Burroughs, age six at this writing—have been on a mission trip with their parents in Africa, working with World Vision and making a difference in the lives of families in Malawi, Africa! Walker, of course, is a major "hit" with the African children because he is a bright redhead—and most of them have never seen such!

Believing God helps us look forward, knowing and trusting God for the future. As Bible teacher/biblical scholar Beth Moore says, "God is who He says He is and can do what He says He can do."

Contemporary Faithful Women

In the study of God's Word, I am constantly amazed at God's plan, from eternity, to know His children and intervene in their lives—calling them to Himself. In doing so, we truly find our stories in God's story. My challenge is to live in such a way that my story is God's story.

A group of women acted out their faith-journey, using hammers, saws, and elbow grease to touch another generation. Wanda Lee, executive director of WMU, writes in her column in *Missions Mosaic* magazine of her 1989 experience in participating in the annual Jimmy Carter Habitat Building, Pikeville, KY.

> *"I was invited to participate in an all-women project as we built a house known as the 'First Ladies House.' The work force consisted of forty women, including the governor's wife of Kentucky, a senator's wife, former First Lady Rosalynn Carter, then-First Lady Hillary Clinton, and other professional women. The house was to be built for a young single mom and her 9-year-old son. One day, I painted next to a 75-year-old retired teacher who was working on her 14th house since retirement. We were a diverse group of women—united around a common goal. I will never forget standing in that small living room with those 40 women singing "Amazing Grace" as Rosalynn Carter presented a Bible to this young mother and her son."*

Lee says of her experience,

> *"I learned the value of teamwork. It has proven true that what we can do together far outweighs what any one of us can do alone. When we join our collective knowledge and experience in the faith together, a lost world will be able to see Christ living in us and be open to hear the truth of His saving grace."*

I can't help but think that these women will continue to tell this story of faithfulness to their children, grandchildren, nieces, and nephews, while leaving a legacy of faithful service, engravings of God's faithfulness.

Faith Impacts Community

On His way to the cross, Jesus lived in community—teaching and touching lives. Matthew 9:18–26 tells of one woman's life He touched. Matthew gives the account of Jesus healing a woman who had faith enough to reach out and touch the hem of His garment. I don't know what this woman heard about Jesus, but it was just enough for her to believe He was who He said He was!

I love this story. Jesus is walking along teaching His disciples.

> *"While He spoke these things to them, behold, a ruler came and worshiped Him, saying, 'My daughter has just died, but come and lay Your hand on her and she will live.' So Jesus arose and followed him, and so did His disciples. And suddenly* [you always know something is going to happen when the Scripture says "suddenly"], *a woman who had a flow of blood for twelve years came from behind and touched the hem of His garment."*

I have to say it did not matter where she touched His garment, His power was His power! And her faith in His power was what gave her the courage—being a woman and an unclean woman at that—to reach out in total belief. Mark 5:28–31 gives a little more insight that is so important to my faith.

> *"For she said, 'If only I may touch His clothes, I shall be made well.' Immediately the fountain of her blood was dried up, and she felt in her body that she was healed of the affliction. And Jesus, immediately* [that's very much like "suddenly"] *knowing in Himself that the power had gone out of Him, turned around in the crowd and said, 'Who touched My clothes?' But His disciples said to Him, 'You see the multitude thronging You, and You say, 'Who touched Me?'"*

I think I would give the disciples a D– on this test! After all, they were going with Him to heal the ruler's daughter. So how come they didn't believe He felt the woman's touch in the crowd? Well…back to the story. Verses 32–34: *"And He looked around to see her who had done this thing."* She is behind His back, but He knows it is a woman. *"But the woman, fearing and trembling, knowing what had happened to her, came and fell down before Him and told Him the whole truth. And He said to her, 'Daughter, your faith has made you well. Go in peace, and be healed of your affliction.'"*

Surely the woman with the issue of blood must have gasped when the Rabbi called her "daughter." Jesus, true to Himself, engraves the heart of this woman with His time and care. His disciples saw the multitude, but Jesus saw the one who came for healing and called her *daughter*.

Touching Jesus' clothes did not heal this woman. It was her faith in His power. He assured her that she was healed from her sickness and sent her away in peace. "Healed" in Greek is *sozo*, which means "saved." What a faith step she took that day. I think Jesus is still looking for that "stretching to reach" kind of faith in women today!

Daughter is an intimate and endearing greeting. Imagine Jesus looking into your eyes and saying, "Daughter." What a moment!

Robert Wolgemuth, in his book *The Most Important Place on Earth,* shares a precious and wonderful tip for parents. Whenever one of his family members walks into the room, they are greeted by name. Each phone call is received with an encouraging greeting, naming the caller, and sharing a delightful greeting. Using a person's name adds significance. What a welcoming thought. I've been trying to do that, and I feel good about it and trust my family does also.

It is Jesus' signature that qualifies us to carry the lamp. Please! Do not fail to pass the *Lamp of God* to this generation...and to the next.

See Jesus stepping into the world...at just the right time...announcing through John 8:12: "*I am the light of the world: He who follows Me shall not walk in darkness, but have the light of life."* How dare we live not being the light in dark places! Paul continues the Lamp tradition and commands, *"For you were formerly darkness, but now you are Light in the Lord; walk as children of Light (for the fruit of the Light consists in all goodness and righteousness and truth), trying to learn what is pleasing to the Lord"* (Ephesians 5:8–10 NASB).

Being the Light in Faithful Living

Between the summer of my freshman and sophomore years in college, I took a job as a waitress in a small restaurant in Asheville, North Carolina. I was new to this kind of work and most of the ladies working there were a good bit older...and a lot more experienced! By nature, I am quite reserved, and back then I was also very shy. I struggled on the job, but did not ask for help. Soon, I was called in by my supervisor and devastated by her reprimand to me: "Just because you are getting a college education does not mean you are one bit better than your coworkers. Don't be so uppity. You need their help and need to be a team player. Besides, I know you are a Christian, so go out there and show it."

I promise...it was my shyness! My lamp must not have been working so well, wouldn't you agree? I should have been singing, "Give me oil in my lamp! Keep it burning!"

Living faith as a *covenant woman* means letting your light shine, no matter what the circumstances. Don't ever forget your inheritance in Him, who is the light of the world. Believe me, I have messed up many times, but I still try to be glowing with the light of Christ.

On another occasion, I had to take a city bus to my high school. When I boarded the bus, I gave the driver $1.00 for the ticket. He gave me the ticket and my change. (It was a lot cheaper then to ride the bus.) When I sat down, I realized he had given me too much change! When the bus arrived at the school, I went to the front and handed the overcharge to the driver saying, "Sir, you gave me too much change." He smiled and looked at me and said: "I know I did. I did it on purpose. You are the preacher's kid and I wanted to see what you'd do with it."

Whew! I passed that test! You see, we are God's kids...children of faith, everyday faith, living God's light in our world. Remember whose child you are. My parents' constant and consistent reminder to their five children was this: "Never forget you are a Milligan!" Certainly, our heavenly Father constantly reminds us: "Remember...you are Mine!"

God's engraved invitation to you...

> ...from a cross
> > ...given to an eternal inheritance
> > > ...signed by Jesus
> > > > ...sealed by the Holy Spirit
> > > > > ...autographed in the Lamb's book...forever!

Now, dear friends...that is a *signature* piece!

Legacies

⤳ OF FAITH

- *Begin now having a family altar time regularly. Read the Bible together, pray together, talk about God's work in your lives, count answers to prayer.*

- *Bless your children 8 times today through touch, words, smiles.*

- *Send yearly Christmas cards/scrapbooks from birth through high school.*

- *Send yearly photos of each child enclosed in love note, and a prayer of blessing for the child.*

- *Write monthly handwritten letters to children, sharing your (and their) faith story.*

- *Take your children to church regularly. Sit together. Hold hands during prayers.*

- *Hum hymns around the house. You'll be surprised what a lifelong impact it can have!*

Resources

1. *Treasures of a Grandmother's Heart: Finding Pearls of Wisdom in Everyday Moments* by Esther Burroughs, published by New Hope Publishers

2. *Growing Kids God's Way: Biblical Ethics for Parenting* by Gary Ezzo, published by Micah 6:8

3. *Daily Light Journal: A Bible Study for Busy People* by Anne Graham Lotz, published by J. Countryman

4. *Missions Mosaic* magazine, published by WMU

5. *The Most Important Place on Earth: What a Christian Home Looks Like and How to Build One* by Robert Wolgemuth, published by Nelson Books

Legacies of Love

While serving on the mission staff of a large denomination in the 1980s, I was invited to be the keynote speaker for a North Carolina Youth Conference. At that time, my office assignment was to challenge young people to "missional living" in community. My task for this conference was to prepare the North Carolina leaders to help their young people "get their hands dirty" on behalf of the under-resourced in their state and in our nation. I love speaking to youth because their response is always so positive. There is nothing they will not attempt. My heart is always encouraged by their contagious enthusiasm.

The conference host gave me the theme and explained that we would celebrate each night in worship beginning with the creation story, moving through Christmas, Easter, and the Resurrection. As I listened to his heart, I immediately felt comfortable with the topics I was to speak on for each session...except the crucifixion story. I told him that I had never delivered a message on the cross and would need some help. "I will pray," he promised. I was looking for a little more help than that...like a borrowed message. It did not happen.

Stewing at my office desk, which was at that time in our home, I had finished all my preparation—except the Thursday night crucifixion story. Almost in desperation, I closed myself away in my bedroom. I read the story of Christ's last week in each of the four Gospels, in every translation I owned.

Mark 15:16–20 tells the story.

> *"Then the soldiers led Him away into the hall called Praetorium, and they called together the whole garrison. And they clothed Him with purple; and they twisted a crown of thorns, put it on His head, and began to salute Him, 'Hail, King of the Jews!' Then they struck Him on the head with a reed and spat on Him; and bowing the knee, they worshiped Him. And when they*

had mocked Him, they took the purple off Him,
put His own clothes on Him, and led Him out to
crucify Him."

I quietly began to sob. What abuse He took for me. I sobbed for those who spit on His face, those who mocked Him, those who beat Him…and for myself…my sin, which put Him on that cross. I have no idea how long I laid on my face, weeping in thankfulness. Never before had I experienced this utter awareness of His grace in my life. I only remember saying over and over, "Thank You, Jesus. Thank You, Jesus." My heart was recaptured by His love and grace.

My thought was: if His story so deeply touched my life, why not just read His story to the students? No wonder Paul says, in Ephesians 6:17: *"And take the helmet of salvation, and the sword of the Spirit, which is the word of God."*

The writer of Hebrews 4:12 reminds us: *"For the word of God is living and powerful, and sharper than any two-edged sword, piercing even to the division of soul and spirit, and of joints and marrow, and is a discerner of the thoughts and intents of the heart."*

I felt His sword that day, cutting away all that was not clean in my life with the presence of His sacrificial love. It was an overwhelming experience of His encounter and presence in my life. I shall never forget it.

Some time later, I came back downstairs to my office. My husband called out to me from his adjacent office, saying, "Did you have a good nap?" I quietly responded, "No, but my heart is renewed."

I went to the conference with no message prepared. As I met with the worship planning team about Thursday night's message, I told them "I would like to sit on a stool and slowly read the crucifixion story." Immediately the drama leader began to smile. They had prepared a drama about the cross! "Esther," he said, "We don't want to tell you the plan! You just keep reading...slowly. Don't react. Just read the story." For the first time since the invitation, I began to joyfully anticipate Thursday worship, trusting God's presence.

The time came. I walked to the stage, took my place on the stool, and said, "Please hear a story that changed my life." I began to read. Silence reigned supreme. From the corner of my eye, I could see a "Christ figure" moving down the right aisle, dragging a large wooden cross and stumbling under its weight. About halfway up the aisle, the young people began to stir. The Christ figure breathed out these words: "Won't anyone here help me carry this cross?" My heart pounded! I could help...but they'd told me not to react, but to keep on reading.

When the Christ figure crossed the front on the auditorium, I was close enough to touch him, and he stumbled again. I nearly fell off the stool—wanting to reach out to him. I caught myself and continued to read...as he spoke again those words, inviting someone to help him carry the cross.

Words through tears.

Love through his cross.

Who would help him?

The journey seemed endless as he made his way up the left aisle. I wondered, *How will this end?* As I came to the close of the Scripture, one last time, he dropped the cross and cried out, "Won't anybody here help me carry this cross?" By then, I was hanging onto that stool with all my might—while my heart wept to help him carry the cross.

At that moment, a young woman stood up in the audience (as part of the drama) and said, "I want to help you, Jesus, but this is my senior year and I have so much ahead of me." Another voice spoke: "I want to help you, Jesus, but I am headed to seminary to prepare for ministry; when I get finished, then I'll help you."

I was dying inside! I wanted to help him, but as I was thinking this, another person stood to make excuse...as we watched the Christ figure depart the building. Then, quietly, a voice from the back began to sing:

Must Jesus bear the cross alone,
And all the world go free?
No; there's a cross for everyone,
And there's a cross for me.

That was it for me! I jumped off the stool (I was much younger then), stepped off the stage, and began calling after him, "I'll help you, Jesus. I'll help you, Jesus!" (This was *not* part of the drama! This must have been the continuation of the day I'd cried with Jesus about His cross.)

Immediately, all over the room, students began standing and quietly moving to the exits. When we left the auditorium, we could see three crosses on a hill. Slowly, the crowd gathered. We stood beneath the cross.

Silence engulfed us.

Truth pierced us.

The message healed us.

And a single voice began a whispered melody: "Amazing grace, how sweet the sound...."

The next morning in the staff meeting, I was told that many sang and wept into the early morning hours. I wonder today, after all these years, how the kingdom has been changed by the signature of the cross, engraved indelibly on the lives of those North Carolina teenagers. Certainly eternity will give voice to all those stories of God's love engraving students of that generation.

Passing the Baton

My challenge today to my readers is to live in light of eternity, imprinting another generation—carrying the cross, if you please. Each new generation desperately needs "baton passers" to complete the race for eternity in victory.

I remember watching the 2004 Olympic relay races and seeing the USA teams struggle to pass the baton successfully. This time they failed to receive the gold. It reminds me of God's long ago instruction to His team.

Carefully read aloud this paraphrase of Psalm 78:1–8 from *The Message* by Eugene Peterson:

"Listen, dear friends, to God's truth,
    bend your ears to what I tell you.
I'm chewing on the morsel of a proverb;
    I'll let you in on the sweet old truths,
Stories we heard from our fathers,
    counsel we learned at our mothers' knee.
We're not keeping this to ourselves,
    we're passing it along [the baton] *to the next*
    generation—
GOD's fame and fortune,
    the marvelous things he has done.

He planted a witness in Jacob,
    set his Word firmly in Israel,
Then commanded our parents
    to teach it to their children
So the next generation would know,
    and all generations to come—
Know the truth and **tell the stories**
    so their children can trust in God,
Never forget the works of God
    but keep his commands to the letter.
Heaven forbid they should be like their parents,
    bullheaded and bad,
A fickle and faithless bunch
    who never stayed true to God."

The cross is God's "signature piece"—His nail-scarred, thorn-crowned, blood-bought signature, engraving *extravagant* love on our lives. His signature engraves our invitation to eternal life, and eternal living. You must RSVP! I love the thought from Isaiah 49:16 (AMP) that God has *"tattooed a picture"* of me on both of His hands. I want to engrave on my heart His nail-pierced handprint and never ever forget the cost.

May I challenge you, my dear reader, to eternal living, living and leaving a heritage that impacts eternity? As the old song says, "This world is not my home, we're just a-passing through." So as you pass through, engrave a spiritual legacy that you may become a blessing to generations yet to be born. Live in the expectation of your eternal home. The Word tells us in Luke 12:32–34 (TLB), *"So don't be afraid, little flock. For it gives your Father great happiness to give you the Kingdom. Sell what you have and give to those in need. This will fatten your purses in heaven! And the purses of heaven have no rips or holes in them. Your treasure there will never disappear; no thief can steal them; no moth can destroy them. Wherever your treasure is, there your heart and thoughts will also be."*

Think kingdom! Live to make a difference in the lives of those whom you would like to be at the marriage feast of the Lamb, when He Himself will seat us, put on a waiter's uniform, and serve us.

In his Gospel, Luke tells us how to live in light of eternity by quoting Jesus: *"If anyone desires to come after Me, let him deny himself, and take up his cross daily, and follow Me. For whoever desires to save his life will lose it, but whoever loses his life for My sake will save it"* (Luke 9:23–24).

What will we do with this invitation? Let me suggest that we must intentionally share this engraved invitation with yet another generation, be it your own family, your neighborhood family, your workplace family, your church family, or your spiritual family. We earn the right to be heard when we deny ourselves and take up our cross daily and follow.

In Genesis 15:18, we hear these words: *"On the same day the Lord made a covenant (promise, pledge) with Abram, saying, To your descendants I have given this land, from the river of Egypt to the great river Euphrates"* (AMP). What a promise to a couple who, at the time, had no descendants! Our heritage began with God's promise to Abraham, God's covenant with Israel. Jesus became our new covenant—engraving His love through His death, marking you, deeply engraving your life with His life.

A Word of Truth

What God promises, He is able to perform. In Romans 4:21, Paul writes about God's promise to Abraham, to make him the father of many nations. Abraham and Sarah were both past ninety! Impossible! I'm sure I too would have perhaps laughed at God's promise. I'm sure I too would have tried to make it happen through my power, just as Abraham and Sarah did. Have you noticed the difference between when you take your life and circumstances in your hands and when you trust God's promises? One is all about you, the other all about Him. There is a huge difference. When it is about God, it brings glory to God. When it is about me, it's about me. We learn the importance of living "in Him" from 2 Corinthians 1:20–22. *The Message* says it this way:

> *"Whatever God has promised gets stamped [engraved] with the Yes of Jesus. In him, this is what we preach and pray, the great Amen, God's Yes and our Yes together, gloriously evident. God affirms us, making us a sure thing in Christ, putting his Yes within us. By his Spirit he has stamped [engraved] us with His eternal pledge—a sure beginning of what he is destined to complete."*

Don't laugh when God makes a promise! What God promises, He is able to perform. You are joint heirs with Christ Jesus, and that makes you God's inheritance!

A Word to Live By

Leave a godly heritage! Leave a spiritual inheritance. God's Word commands us to pass on the stories we have heard from our fathers, and the counsel we learned at our mother's knee (Psalm 78).

The words *heritage* and *legacy* have very similar meanings, according to Webster's Dictionary: "Something transmitted by or acquired from a predecessor; tradition." I am glad that the tradition passed on doesn't just include ancestors, but can include almost anyone who came before. I like that. It helps me realize I have a responsibility to live intentionally with everyone I meet, passing on traditions and stories to those coming behind me. Believe it!

Shaped By Our Stories

We are shaped by our stories. Some time back, I attended a family reunion in Canada honoring my father and his only living sibling, Aunt Mary, who at that time were both in their mid-90s. We learned much about our "Milligan" story at that reunion. My father's parents moved from Ireland and became homesteaders in Alberta, Canada. They were very religious people. They helped build the roads, helped build the one-room school house, and helped build, of course, the church. But it was not until my father, a schoolteacher in the farm community, was 27 years old that he heard the gospel in a small downtown Baptist Church. At that time, he was dating the woman who would become my mother. They both came to know Christ. My dad says, "I went to pick up your mother for church on a Sunday morning. Before we left for church, we knelt down at mother's home and prayed, telling God we wanted to be saved." That Sunday morning, they came forward to the altar, forever altering their lives.

Soon after he came to know Christ, my father heard God's call to the ministry as a pastor. He and my mother set off to attend a Bible college to prepare themselves for ministry. Mother had a seventh-grade education, but she also attended Bible school for one year before they married. She became a serious student of God's Word. My brothers, sisters, and I were "marked" by our mother's love of the Word of God. She lived her life according to God's Word.

I have fond memories of her with her Bible open as she read and prayed. Mother's prayer journals record that 48 family members came to know Christ because she and my daddy shared with both their families. My father's family moved from being a "religious" family to being a "converted" family.

At this same family reunion, each grandchild had been asked to write a letter of a "story of influence" that had come from Uncle Dave (my father) and Aunt Mary. Each of his nieces and nephews shared how my father, their uncle, had led them to pray to receive Christ. Talk about leaving a legacy!

A Word of Caution!

Strong family traditions must be built intentionally. Today's scattered culture does not lend itself to traditions, stories, or gatherings. But tradition can be started in any family at any time. It is never too late.

Early in my childhood, parents instructed and corrected children. Teachers and neighbors did the same. If we misbehaved at school, we were punished at home. If we were mischievous in town or at the park, we were corrected and reported to our parents by caring neighbors or relatives, and we were disciplined at home. The little community of Crossfield, Alberta, Canada, helped raise its children. Perhaps it really does take a village to raise a child! I got the message that I belonged to my family and also to my community family.

No matter how often we get together as siblings, we tell our stories over and over, laughing and crying about our legacy. A tradition we still carry on is family games. I read with interest an article in *USA Today* not long after the 9/11 tragedy in New York City: toy stores across the nation reported a huge increase in the purchase of board games. It was indeed a time for families to pull close together. I could hope that some families made game night a tradition. How sad that it took a tragedy to help families see the importance of playing together.

Every Friday night of my childhood, we celebrated family night. On that night, everyone had a job in preparing the dinner table. A tablecloth and the "good dishes" were set. It was an event. After dinner, everyone helped clear the table to get ready for table games. The evening was concluded as each child played a selection on their instrument, or recited Scripture or poetry. Then we gathered around the radio and listened to *Fibber McGee and Molly*. How we would laugh with our radio friends. How we argued over our games. How we—I—dreaded the piano recital time, but today I know our parents were passing on the "leadership baton," giving expression to our talents and abilities. No! I don't play the piano today in public, but I do play it for my own joy, pleasure, and spiritual renewal. When my heart is hurting, I eventually make my way to our piano. I sing as I play hymns, restoring my heart in God's love and care.

Bob and I carried to our home the "family night" tradition. For us, family night included games, good food, family altar, playing, and praying together. I've seen the bumper sticker, *The family that prays together stays together,* and I would add *and plays together.* So much is learned as families play together. Personalities emerge. Winners and losers learn to deal with defeat and victory in an acceptable manner. Team spirit is developed. Life lessons are learned. Pass the baton of family traditions that will become legacies for another generation. If you did not receive family traditions, it isn't too late to begin them. You will bless another generation. Don't drop this baton!

A Word of Promise

God's promises may be fulfilled in your descendants and your spiritual offspring. Live believing God's promises. Live for eternity.

Not everyone receives an inheritance, but everyone can leave a legacy. It is the life you live. The greatest legacy you can leave another generation is God's love story in your life. Tell your faith story. Deuteronomy 4:9–10 warns us, "*Only take heed to yourself, and diligently keep yourself, lest you forget the things your eyes have seen, and lest they depart from your heart all the days of your life. And teach them to your children and your grandchildren, especially concerning the day you stood before the* LORD *your God in Horeb, when the* LORD *said to me, 'Gather the people to Me, and I will let them hear My words, that they may learn to fear Me all the days they live on the earth, and that they may teach their children.'"*

> *Not everyone receives an inheritance, but everyone can leave a legacy. It is the life you live.*

As I am writing this chapter, I am also Nana-sitting our grand-twins, who started kindergarten in the fall of 2004. I follow their parents' bedtime traditions, which include bath time, story time, prayer time, and "kisses all around." When I started to walk out of Milligan's bedroom tonight, she said, "Nana, my daddy always does this before he goes down the stairs." Having said that, she signed the words, *I love you* and then blew me a kiss. She continued: "You need to practice this Nana so you can do it right. Now try it, Nana." I did. "That's just gweat! Nana, it's all about love and safety." I thought: *How precious! A parent assuring a child of love and safety as she falls off to sleep.*

I smiled as I thought, *She will grow through the years in the safety of her parents' love being signed to her at bedtime.*

It will be deeply engraved on her heart by the time she leaves home. How wonderful it must feel as a child to receive a gift of love and safety.

Now, jump ahead with me to the day Milligan has her own child. Don't you know she will pass on that nighttime ritual and love legacy to her child? That would be my great-grandchild—and the story goes on and on and on. Rituals become legacies, touching generations yet to be born.

There's more...so much more. From the beginning, God created us for Himself. The heavenly Father's promises are even dearer than a parent's promises. Long before Jesus carried that cross that became your eternal inheritance, God promised to counsel you. Pause, and quietly let these Scriptures sink deeply into your heart. This is our precious legacy!

> *"You are a hiding place for me;*
> *You, Lord, preserve me from trouble,*
> *You surround me with songs and shouts of deliverance.*
>
> *I [the Lord] will instruct you and teach you in the way you should go;*
> *I will counsel you with My eye upon you."*
> —Psalm 32:7–8 (AMP)
>
> *"I will bless the LORD who has counseled me;*
> *Indeed, my mind instructs me in the night."*
> —Psalm 16:7 (NASB)

"Yours is the day, Yours also is the night."
                              —Psalm 74:16 (NASB)

"[You] *declare Your lovingkindness in the morning,*
    And Your faithfulness every night."
                                        —Psalm 92:2

"Keep me as the apple of Your eye;
    Hide me under the shadow of Your wings."
                                    —Psalm 17:8

"For the LORD's portion is His people [That's us, beloved];
    Jacob is the allotment of His inheritance.
He found him in a desert land [He found me there, also]…
He encircled him, He cared for him,
    He guarded him as the pupil of His eye.
Like an eagle that stirs up its nest,
    That hovers over its young,
He spread His wings and caught them,
    He carried them on His pinions.
The LORD alone guided him."
                        —Deuteronomy 32:9–12 (NASB)

"He will give His angels charge
concerning you,
    To guard you in all your ways."
                                    —Psalm 91:11

"O Love that
wilt not let me go,
I rest my weary soul in Thee;
I give Thee back the life
I owe, That in Thine ocean
depths its flow
May richer, fuller be."
—*George Matheson*

Beloved, God is standing at your heart's door and signing "I love you"—blowing you a kiss! Teach it to your children, and to everyone within your circle of influence, so that they will know the Father's wonderful love, deep in their hearts, and never forget it.

Legacies

∞ OF LOVE

- *Have tea parties with children and dolls or stuffed animals.*

- *Take time to begin reading a children's chapter book with your kids, a chapter at a time.*

- *Plan an overnight campout in your back yard.*

- *Write a love note to a grandparent or adopted grandparent.*

- *Make an art gallery of your children's art on your garage wall.*

- *Sponge paint a child's hand, or paint the handprint on the laundry room wall.*

- *Record children reading for memory's sake.*

- *Hug your children regularly.*

- *Develop a special goodnight routine that lets children feel secure and loved.*

chapter three

Legacies of
Joy

*S*aturday night I announced my plans for taking family photos on Sunday morning before we left for church. Our daughter Melody was nine and David was five at the time. It worked. Everyone was ready. David kept looking me over that morning. I was wearing for the first time a home-made brown dress, one I was proud of, and a matching wide-brimmed hat. Hands on his hips, he asked, "Are you going to wear that to church?" I nod-ded, fully expecting a compliment, when he announced, "Well, your hat's crooked and you look like Old McDonald." I don't know about you, but I've had some crooked hat days and some Old McDonald days in my lifetime. I laugh now at my son's honesty. Humor is a great gift. Laugh often—lighten up—live in His joy!

Humor is a great gift. Laugh often—lighten up—live in His joy!

When my husband Bob retired from his career as a church musician in 2001, we moved to Birmingham, Alabama. We closed on our new home on December 21, so we did not have time to move in and decorate the house for Christmas. For a variety of reasons, Christmas 2004 was the first Christmas in three years that we decorated our home! I was so very excited. I am just like a little child when it comes to Christmas. We purchased a new tree—and cheated with one that has permanent lights to make it easier for us. This kind of tree is quite a departure for me. I grew up going to the Canadian woods with my Daddy…in the snow…to cut down a real pine tree and drag it home on a bobsled! But hey! In my season of life, *simpler is better*. We still struggled getting all those branch numbers connected and plugging in the right sockets so all the lights would work. It was quite a feat. At one point, Bob was ready to call it quits! We prevailed and we finally made it work.

Our new tree was, indeed, beautiful! We wanted the twins (at that time five years old) to come over to help us decorate the tree. The evening was planned. We would decorate the tree in the afternoon and their parents would join us after work for dinner. With great delight, I unpacked the Christmas decorations and ornament boxes, getting them ready for the twins' arrival.

Christmas music fills our home from the Friday of Thanksgiving until after Christmas. After all, I live with a church musician/composer. Preparing for the twins' arrival, the fragrance of hot chocolate and cookies filled the air. When they arrived, we began decorating. My habit through many years has been to wrap each ornament in tissue paper and store them in labeled boxes. Bob and I laughed in delight as Milligan and Walker unwrapped each ornament—as if each one was a gift—for our lighted tree in celebration of the greatest gift ever given. "Look at all these presents!" They kept saying. "Who is this present for, Nana?"

We have collected ornaments in our travels from all over the world. When we travel, one of my traditions is to bring the children and grandchildren a Christmas ornament from the country we visit.

Children bring such joy to Christmas! Don't you agree? They are too little and uninhibited to mask their delight. They laugh and sing so freely—just because it's in their hearts. I'm told that children laugh some 200 times a day. Adults laugh only about 15 times a day. Guess who's having the best time in life? Our joy, added to the joy of the grandtwins, made a happy occasion for us. Their joy at the end of the decorating task was as strong as when they began. In fact, they kept touching and asking about each ornament as they placed each one on the tree.

Well into the decorating process, I was surprised to realize that the twins had placed every ornament at their arms' height, and all the ornaments were right in the center front of the tree! My "Type A" personality thought for a split second: "They have just decorated one part of the tree!" I am so happy to tell you God is changing my personality Type A to a Type B. I smiled. Laughed out loud, really. I did not change a single ornament placed on that tree. (Later Bob and I put other decorations at the back of the tree.)

Joy is experienced as we delight in life gifts that we see, feel, and experience. Dear Reader, receive joy as a gift. It is, you know! Consider the Source of real joy. Next to our salvation and certainly connected to it, Jesus gives us this remarkable gift: **His joy!** In John 15:11, Jesus is speaking to His disciples, saying,

> *"I have told you these things, that My joy and delight may be in you, and that your joy and gladness may be of full measure and complete and overflowing."* (AMP)

The New American Standard Bible says it this way: "...*that My joy may be in you, and that your joy may be made full.*"

The Living Bible says this: "*You will be filled with my joy. Yes, your cup of joy will overflow!*"

We must take this verse in the context. Jesus had been teaching His disciples about the relationship between the vine and the branch. He reminded them: "*live in Me, and let Me live in you*" (John 15:4 TLB).

Then He warns: "*For a branch can't produce fruit when severed from the vine. Nor can you be fruitful apart from me.... For apart from me you can't do a thing*" (John 15:4–5 TLB).

Have you tried to serve Christ all by yourself? I have. That simply means that I do not fully trust Him. Joy and obedience are always linked in Kingdom citizenship.

His Joy

Each morning after breakfast this year, Bob and I have been reading Calvin Miller's devotional book, *Until He Comes*. Then we pray together, and you would be right to guess this to be one of my greatest joys. In this devotional book, Miller writes each devotional thought as if Jesus were speaking directly to us. We have found this book very inspiring and challenging. This November morning, Bob had taken my car to be serviced, so I sat by myself at the kitchen table and read Day #313—and I just have to share it with you.

The Scripture passage is Matthew 28:5–6:

> "*The angel said to the women, 'Do not be afraid; for I know that you are looking for Jesus who has*

*been crucified. He is not here, for He has risen,
just as He said. Come, see the place where He was
lying'"* (NASB).

Speaking through Calvin Miller's pen, Jesus says: "The
women were bringing spices for My burial. They were also
weeping, the best evidence that they meant well. Tears
come when the face is toward the ground. It's a pity, too.
For God can manage things born far above a downcast
spirit. Bring Me no burial spices. I am alive. I can manage
your broken affairs. Look up! See Me! I am at the right
hand of my father. I am alive forevermore. **I have won
joy, and I place this prize inside you**" (The bolding is my
emphasis).

There it is, my friends. Get this truth. Joy is placed in you
and me by Christ himself.

Miller continues:

> *"'He is risen!' was the shout heard around the
> world. The weeping women met an angel. Then
> they heard the words that the mind cannot con-
> tain. And finding out that I was alive, they
> entered a glorious and befuddling state of grace.
> Who could tell of their delirium? **They were
> mad with joy!** What were they to do? Tell it, they
> must. They had to surrender their sanity and tell
> the world they have met an angel. Bit by bit, the
> group insanity filters in from all quarters. They
> are laughing, crying, whispering, and shouting.*

That's how it is when dead men come alive too suddenly. Yet in this marvelous and hysterical truth, there is a new and powerful force loose. **The joy can never be contained.** *If you see an angel, go ahead and tell your friends. Tell your friends. Some will doubt it and be condemned; others will come to the party of the mad and gain life eternal. Let them doubt your sanity but not your commitment. I am the Lord. 'I am the Alpha and the Omega,' says the Lord God, 'who is, and who was and who is to come, the Almighty.' (Revelation 1:18) Is this not the grandest, most glorious insanity the world has ever known?"*

What a way to live, no matter our age—living from His joy in us. I want to live like that, dear Jesus, letting Your joy in me spill out in my circle of influence. Living… mad with joy! I am thinking our mistake is that we think of joy as being ours—something we have to work up—something we have to make happen. My prayer for you is that you will begin to live knowing that the joy is His to give, and He does with such purpose.

I want to live like that, dear Jesus, letting Your joy in me spill out in my circle of influence. Living…mad with joy!

Never forget that He paid a great price for your joy. Then He placed this gift in you. It is His joy in you, making it your joy in Him. John's Gospel reminds us that He puts His joy in us so our joy will be full. Why do we see a lack of joy in homes and in the body of Christ? Could it be that we are trying to trump up our own joy, running to every "Christian event" always looking for a fresh encounter …rather than running to and abiding in Christ, soaking up time in His Word, living in the joy of His presence in us? You have the prize. He died to give it to you. It's a legacy that must be shared!

The late Carolyn Rhea, beloved wife of Dr. Claude Rhea, writing in *Glimpses of God's Presence*, says, "Laughter oils life's squeaking joints! Could it be that God, who stocked life's shelves with laughter, stands nearby laughing with me?" Live in laughter so God can say about you: "Yes, you did laugh. I heard you." Oil your life with His prize: JOY.

The Secret of Joy

Let's look at the context of the teacher's instruction to His disciples in John 15:5:

> *"I am the vine, you are the branches. He who abides in Me, and I in him, bears much fruit; for without Me you can do nothing."*

Verse seven says:

> *"If you abide in Me, and My words abide in you, you will ask what you desire, and it shall be done for you."*

Verses nine and ten:

> *"As the Father loved Me, I also have loved you; abide in My love. If you keep My commandments, you will abide in My love, just as I have kept My Father's commandments and abide in His love."*

Verse eleven:

> *"These things I have spoken to you, that My joy many remain in you, and that your joy may be full."*

Strong's Greek & Hebrew Dictionary's transliteration of the word joy is *chara,* and it means joyfulness, joyous, and gladness.

Joy and abiding are connected, just as the branch is connected to the vine and gets nourishment from the vine. When you and I abide in Christ, we are nourished. Remember: the same nourishment in a tree feeds the trunk, the branch, and ultimately the fruit. Jesus promises to love us as His Father loved Him, and invites us to keep His commands, abide in His love, and relish in His joy.

Bruce Wilkinson, in his insightful little book, *Secrets of the Vine*, says, "Within six verses in John 15, Jesus says 'abide' ten times. You can sense the passion and poignancy of His plea. Jesus knows He is about to leave His friends; yet He is saying, 'We must be together.'" Bruce says that the third secret of the Vine is: "If your life bears a lot of fruit, God will invite you to abide more deeply with Him." What a great reward!

Serving— without joy—means you end up joyless. Serving, out of an abiding friendship with God, is joyful simply because it's His joy placed inside of you— by Him.

Perhaps one of the reasons for lack of joy and celebration in the body of Christ is that we stay so busy "doing things for God" that we fill our lives with activities such as church, ministry, family, and we forget the One who invites us to His presence to abide in His love. Serving—without joy—means you end up joyless. Serving, out of an abiding friendship with God, is joyful simply because it's His joy placed inside of you— by Him. Bruce Wilkinson also says, "Abiding is all about the most important friendship of your life. In abiding, you seek, long, thirst, wait, see, know, love, hear, and respond to…a Person. More abiding means more of God in your life, more of Him in your activities, thoughts, and desires."

In our current culture we rush to do, to go, and to perform—thinking we are pleasing God—when what He truly desires is that we simply enjoy His company. Author John Piper in his book *Desiring God* says: "God is most glorified in me when I am most satisfied in Him. You might turn your world on its head by changing one word in your creed. The old tradition says 'The chief end of man is to glorify God *and* enjoy Him forever.'" Piper's premise for his book is this: The chief end of man is to glorify God *by* enjoying Him forever.

Consider abiding as "enjoying God" and being filled with Christ's empowering presence. Joyful living should be a pleasant, delightful life journey, even when embracing pain. Enjoy God. He delights in you. He sings over you. He dances over you with joy, as proclaimed in the Jerusalem Bible. Join Him!

My friend, Jolene Ivey, a woman who is just full of life and joy, says it takes 72 muscles to frown and only 15 muscles to smile. Work those smile muscles to the glory of God! Laughter can be:

- a peacemaker
- a bridge builder
- a defuser of conflict
- a health improvement
- a life enhancer

Oswald Chambers says, "The last mark of intimacy is to confide secret joys. Psalm 24:14 says: Have we ever let God tell us any of His joys or are we telling God our secrets so continually that we leave no room for Him to talk to us? The things that make God dear to us are not so much His great big blessings as the tiny things, because they show His amazing intimacy with us; He knows every detail of our individual lives."

Joyful Encounters

OK, who in your life is the most joyful person? You probably know immediately. Jot this name in the margin of this page. Now, give thanks for this person and the joy they bring to your life. Are you smiling? I am! I know my "joy person!" A joyful person pulls you into the presence of Jesus, our joy-giver. They are contagious and refreshing, are they not?

My friend and mentor, Marge Caldwell, is certainly one of God's most joyful saints. I first met her in the mid-1960s at a house party on the Baylor University campus. During her message, I laughed until I cried. She was the funniest and most joyful Christian I'd ever seen or heard. She was *in love with* Jesus, and it showed! Listening to her speak made me want to be in love with Jesus with all my heart.

She also loved her husband dearly and fondly called him "Chuckie." In those days, not many people in church ever talked much about love or romance. Marge did—and young women loved it because she was so real and spoke from God's word to their hearts.

Marge made living so much fun. She was so full of joy. My heart was full after hearing her the first time. I honestly did not know that Christians could have that much fun. I wanted to get in her pocket and go home with her to see if her joy could rub off on me.

I was convicted that perhaps I was not much fun as a mother. She made me want to be. My childhood church experience was not about *joyful living*, but rather, *dutiful living*, and let me tell you—it showed on every face!

In the last 15 years, it has been my joy to plan conferences for women. I've had the honor of inviting Marge to be a keynote speaker several times. I never dreamed that Marge and I would speak on the same program!

A few years ago, we were speaking together and were assigned to be roommates. I laughed out loud as she wrapped her hair in bathroom tissue each night then sat on her bed writing in her journal to God. She'd burst out laughing and read me what she had just written. Being her roommate was like being in the scene in the movie *Mary Poppins* where the uncle flies up in the air every time he starts laugh. Marge was teaching me to lighten up, laugh more, releasing God's joy. It was not *lecture* learning. It was just how she did life…in His joy. Dear Reader, how I wish I'd learned that much earlier in life! If I could do parenting over again, I'd do the "laughter thing" right the second time.

I'm thinking that God knew He would have to give us the gift of grandparenting so we could have another chance. Grandparenting is just that: grand. We are on the outside looking in…with love. We've learned to laugh with deep joy, to cherish all the silly, wonderful, delightful moments of life that carry us through life's difficult times.

Grandparenting means:

- blessing the family needs
- being encouraging teachers
- becoming the cheering section for the grandkids
- encouraging the next generation to live joyfully

Parents are also all of these things, but if you are a grandparent, you are that *other* example the grandkids need to see while helping them experience the tradition of joy as part of their legacy. Children should see what God's love is all about through their parents. Remember this, if you came from a joyless environment, don't pass that legacy on. It is never too late to start a laughter-and-joy legacy. Engrave your family life with His joy.

I pray we will pass the *mad with joy* baton to generations to come. Come on now! Grab the prize of joy from Christ and run with that baton. Run the race with great joy! You will find that it is contagious.

God's invitation is to live in unconditional joy. Maybe, like me, you didn't get it the first time because we were too busy trying to do it right. We did not leave much room to live being *mad with joy*, and I fear the present generation may be in an even bigger hurry—not taking time to experience the joy of life.

We better get it right so we will be able to laugh when our grandkids are so honest with us. I was rocking my firstborn granddaughter, Anna Esther, when she was little. At one moment, she reached up, touched my face, and said: "Nana, you are so wrinkled!" Before I could react, she continued: "But they only show when you smile." Well, I am not giving up smiling!

Stress is often the *enemy* of laughter. We find ourselves doing too much...being too serious, and often, just not being much fun. Robert Wolgemuth, in his wonderful book *The Most Important Place on Earth,* says:

Remember this, if you came from a joyless environment, don't pass that legacy on. It is never too late to start a laughter-and-joy legacy. Engrave your family life with His joy.

> *In a family, you may have noticed this yourself: Self-humor is wonderfully contagious. When our children observe our ability and eccentricities, they'll have a pattern to follow for themselves. This results in far less touchiness and fewer broken hearts and angry outbursts...and more fun at home.*

Laughing with God

I am thinking about another woman who laughed, and I am very certain she was very wrinkled. You will find the story in Genesis 18 (NRSV). Verse 1 says:

> *"The LORD appeared to Abraham by the oaks of Mamre, as he sat at the entrance of his tent in the heat of the day."*

Abraham entertained three men and in doing so, obtained a life-changing message from God. Verse 9:

> *"They said to him, 'Where is your wife Sarah?'"*

Notice that the Lord knew her name! *"And he said, 'There, in the tent.' Then one said, 'I will surely return to you in **due season**, and your wife Sarah shall have a son.'"* I love God's specific message. Make no mistake about it, He named Sarah the soon-to-be mother. *"And Sarah was listening at the tent entrance behind him."* (It's a woman thing, to listen in!)

The Scripture tells us that Abraham and Sarah were well past childbearing age. Verse 12:

> *"So Sarah laughed to herself, saying, 'After I have grown old, and my husband is old, shall I have pleasure?'"*

Now, I might also have been laughing to myself. In fact, I might be doubled over in laughter, touching my wrinkled face and body and, yes, laughing out loud at the very thought of bearing a child at that age! Before we are too hard on Sarah, think back about the things God has asked you to do. How often did you laugh to yourself, as Sarah did?

Then comes the dialogue in verse 13: *"The LORD said to Abraham, 'Why did Sarah laugh, and say, 'Shall I indeed bear a child, now that I am old?' Is there anything too wonderful for the LORD? At the set time I will return to you, **in due season,** and Sarah shall have a son.' But Sarah denied, saying, 'I did not laugh'; for she was afraid. He said, 'Oh yes, you did laugh.'"*

I'm smiling as I think how many times women, upon learning a friend is expecting a child, ask, "When are you due?" Sarah would have answered, "In due season."

Joy and Laughter

In 1961, as Bob was finishing his master's degree in church music from Southwestern Seminary, he was contacted by a number of churches who were searching for a minister of music. We had driven from Dennison, Texas, to Tulsa, Oklahoma, to visit such a church. On our way back home, I asked Bob if we could drive by First Baptist Church, Muskogee, Oklahoma. We had been recommended to them and were interested...that is, if they had an interest. Bob agreed, so we drove to Muskogee and found the church on Main

Street. "Let's just go peek in the door and look at the sanctuary," Bob suggested. Excited as little children, we tried the front door and it was open! We entered quietly and took the steps to the balcony. We sat there—holding hands—as we looked around the sanctuary. Then we boldly prayed that if this were the place God wanted us to serve, we would be willing to come. Yes, God knew we had been recommended to the church, we knew the church was a great missions church, and they were without a minister of music.

God's Word says that He knows the end from the beginning (Ecclesiastes 3:11). We left the church as quietly as we entered. I could not stop smiling—thinking how God might answer such an audacious prayer. Several weeks passed ever so slowly.

One Saturday morning, Bob was in Birmingham, Alabama, talking with a church. The phone rang. I answered, and the operator asked for Bob Burroughs. I said, "He is not here, but this is his wife. May I be of help?" The voice on the phone said to the operator, "Just let me talk to her. I want to know what she thinks. Esther, this is Felix Wagoner, pastor of First Baptist Church, Muskogee, Oklahoma."

I gasped!

He continued. "We are looking for a minister of music, and I hear your husband is the man we need." *Gasp!* again. "Do you think your husband would be interested in talking to us?"

OK…I'm nearly dancing by now!

"Yes, sir. I think he would be interested."

I did not dare tell him that we had prayed in their sanctuary a few weeks earlier.

"Now that's the kind of answer I want! I like you already," he laughed loudly. He wanted to know where Bob was and I told him he was interviewing with a church in Alabama.

He said, "When he gets home, you tell him not to take that church until we talk! Now, young lady, let me pray with you about this." He did. "I'll call you back next week. You keep praying," he said as he hung up.

I kept praying and laughing and laughing and praying—not because I was in Sarah's condition, though we were expecting our first child, but because God's timing was in *due season*. I think God was also smiling, watching His children encounter each other. Rev. Felix Wagoner did call the next week and soon thereafter, First Baptist Church of Muskogee, Oklahoma, called Bob Burroughs, fresh out of seminary, as their minister of music and youth.

We eventually did tell our story about praying in the balcony to the pastor. Pastor Wagoner was a man so full of life, humor, and joy. He helped both of us begin enjoying our journey of ministry.

Come on, now! Let's get the joy thing right! Smile, and let the wrinkles be the proof of His joy in you.

Now…back to Sarah.

In due season, her son Isaac, whose name means "Laughter," was born. In Genesis 21:6 (NRSV) the Scripture says, "*Now Sarah said, 'God has brought laughter for me; everyone who hears will laugh with me.'*" What a celebration that must have been!

Some generations later, the Hebrew children were celebrating again in laughter. Psalm 126 (*The Message*) tells this story.

> *"It seemed like a dream, too good to be true, when God returned Zion's exiles. We laughed, we sang, we couldn't believe our good fortune. We were the talk of the nations. 'God was wonderful to them!' God was wonderful to us; we are one happy people. And now, God, do it again; bring rains to our drought-stricken lives so those who planted their crops in despair will shout hurrahs at the harvest, so those who went off with heavy hearts will come home laughing, with armloads of blessing."*

The word *laugh,* according to the Greek/Hebrew Dictionary, means *celebrate, rejoice, frolic, dance, laugh,* and *smile.*

No wonder when Jesus breaks in on the scene, He is enjoying parties, lunching with friends, attending wedding celebrations, and bringing the dead to life. Now, that is **joy** unspeakable and never before experienced in the New Testament church!

It isn't long before this traveling storyteller models for His disciples how to live in His joy. We read in Matthew 8:1–3:

> *"When He had come down from the mountain, great multitudes followed Him. And behold, a*

*leper came and worshipped Him, saying, 'Lord,
if You are willing, You can make me clean.' And
Then Jesus put out His hand and touched him,
saying, 'I am willing; be cleansed.' Immediately
his leprosy was cleansed."*

Jesus is immediately met by a centurion, who asks for healing for his paralyzed servant. Jesus responds, *"I will come
and heal him."* The centurion says, *"For I also am a man
under authority, having soldiers under me. And I say to
this one, 'Go,' and he goes; and to another, 'Come,' and he
comes; and to my servant, 'Do this,' and he does it."* Jesus
is amazed at his great faith. *"Go your way; and as you
have believed, let it be done for you"* (Matthew 8:5-13).

Then, in Peter's home, Jesus saw Peter's mother-in-law
lying ill with a fever. No one asks for a miracle. The Scripture
simply says:

*"So he touched her hand, and the fever left her.
And she arose and served them. When evening
had come, they brought to Him many who were
demon-possessed. And He cast out the spirits
with a word, and healed all who were sick, that
it might be fulfilled which was spoken by Isaiah
the prophet, saying: HE HIMSELF TOOK OUR
INFIRMITIES, AND BORE OUR SICKNESSES."*

—Matthew 8:15–17

I am thinking there was some joyful dancing and celebrating going on here! What a day these followers of Jesus had —seeing His joy in doing what God had sent Him to do. Surely, all heaven sang for joy as they watched the Father's Son. I cannot help but believe that heaven also rejoices when you and I live in joyful obedience to our heavenly Father. It is no wonder that Jesus told His disciples how to be full and overflowing with His joy.

I cannot help but believe that heaven rejoices when you and I live in joyful obedience to our heavenly Father. It is no wonder that Jesus told His disciples how to be full and overflowing with His joy.

Laughter Legacies

I was teaching *Experiencing God*, written by my good friend Henry Blackaby, at a Music Week Conference in North Carolina. My class was made up of spouses of church musicians who were not attending a specific music class. The room was full with folks standing around the room. My husband, Bob, was in the group sitting on a table to my far left. It was a warm June morning, no air conditioning and the room was not just warm...it was hot! Well into teaching the lesson, and because of the heat, I took off my red linen jacket. As I was speaking and turned toward Bob's side of the room, I noticed he was motioning to me in a strange way. I kept speaking, but wondered what on earth he wanted. I looked again, and he was still motioning. It looked for all the world like he was telling me to zip up my zipper!

Before I continue, let me share a memory. Early in our ministry, Bob came to the platform in a church to lead the first hymn. Watching him, I noticed that his fly was unzipped. Picture this now...on the front row, I am making "zipping" motions up and down the front of my skirt! He got the message! Immediately following the hymn, he called for prayer and calmly fixed his problem.

Now it was my turn. Bob was doing his best to get me the message. Finally, I looked down to see my white blouse sticking out of the zipper of my skirt. "Oops," I said, and turned from the audience, tucked in my blouse and as I turned back to the audience, I saw a brown grocery sack on the floor. I leaned over, picked it up, and placed it over my head, saying, "As I was saying...." The room broke into a symphony of laughter and applause. It took several minutes for us to get back on track. It was a joyful moment right in the middle of teaching. I meet people all over the country who remind me they were with me in the conference when I wore the red suit and the brown paper bag. Of course, we laugh all over again.

Learn to enjoy moments of abandoned laughter, knowing God is laughing, too. One of the most consistent needs in today's family is the sound of laughter—healing joy-filled laughter.

Life can rob our joy if we allow it. The four Ps can rob our joy:

People
Places
Possessions
Positions

Don't let them! If we let God provide the balance in our lives, the same four Ps can bring joy. Hold *lightly* to earthly things. Hold *tightly* to things eternal. And in that balance, you will find joy.

Legacies

— OF JOY

- *Fun "family movie" night.*

- *Dinner table—"best joke shared" award.*

- *Family charades...kids love it!*

- *Trivia, riddles, games.*

- *Sticky notes in lunch boxes.*

- *Love notes on pillows.*

- *Begin some new family traditions.*

- *Give children/grandchildren a yearly Christmas ornament.*

- *Bless your children as you put them to bed, yes, even your teens.*

Resources

1. *Until He Comes: Daily Inspirations for Those Who Await the Savior* by Calvin Miller, published by Broadman & Holman Publishers

2. *Glimpses of God's Presence* by Carolyn Rhea, published by Broadman Press

3. *Secrets of the Vine: Breaking Through to Abundance* by Bruce Wilkinson, published by Multnomah Publishers

4. *Desiring God* by John Piper, published by Multnomah Publishers

5. *Experiencing God: Knowing and Doing His Will* by Henry Blackaby, published by Lifeway Press

6. *The Most Important Place on Earth: What a Christian Home Looks Like and How to Build One* by Robert Wolgemuth, published by Nelson Books

Legacies of Hope and Love

When you bless the little children
Generations will be blest.
When you bless the little children
Godly heritage will last.
When you bless the little children
Generations will be blest.
Please bless the little children,
Bless them with faith, hope and love.
  —Bob & Esther Burroughs, 1971

re you looking for *hope* and *encouragement* today? I am so certain that each of the disciples Jesus chose and called to follow Him were often in need of hope and encouragement! How about you and your family? Need hope? Need encouragement? In chapter 1 of this book, we looked at the Author of Faith. In chapter 2, we looked at the Author of Love. And in chapter 3, the Author of Joy. Now we will look at the consummate Giver of Hope.

We need only to look to the Author of Hope and not the empty promises of our current culture. I was in a meeting last year and heard someone say that a major Christian curriculum publisher had conducted a survey among thousands of homes concerning the tradition of family altar. This research resulted in a very disturbing truth. You are going to be surprised at what follows:

> *One half of one percent of the Christian families surveyed opens the Word of God together.*

I was stunned. The Christian home certainly must play the primary role in spiritual formation in the family, teaching, encouraging, and giving reason for hope. Yes, it is a difficult and lifelong task, but it holds the power to engrave the hearts of our children and grandchildren, guiding them toward the Lord for all their days.

Christian families of past generations opened the Bible and prayed together in the home. Granted, we did not have the wonderful resources and Christian education programs to which the churches have access today. The home is God's first created institution...not the church! Parents are given the responsibility to teach their children God's laws, His love and grace.

Hebrews 10:25 instructs, *"Not forsaking or neglecting to assemble together* [as believers] *as is the habit of some people, but admonishing* [warning, urging, and encouraging] *one another, and all the more faithfully as you see the day approaching"* (AMP).

The writer of Hebrews reminds us in verses 23 *and 24* to *"hold fast the confession of our hope without wavering, for He who promised is faithful; and let us consider how to stimulate one another to love and good deeds"* (NASB). We must not forsake our own family opportunities of getting together to encourage one another within the family circle.

This passage is speaking to the body of Christ, but it can also be applied to the family. I heard author and speaker Tony Campolo say, "Traditions and rituals build solidarity in the family. Rituals are the stackpole of traditions that bond and unite families together." In starting our own family traditions, we give place for expressing hope and encouragement in the home.

Encouragement from One Generation to Another

As a new mother, I was not sure of my ability to be a parent. You know the routine. The day arrives. Then you are holding a bundle of softness and thinking, "What do I do next?" Right?

In the '60s, new mothers stayed in the hospital up to five days. It was a great learning time for new parents.

Home—alone—was quite another experience. Yes, believe it or not, cloth diapers had to be dunked in the commode before washing and drying. There was no diaper-smell-free container and no plastic or disposable diapers!

Monday morning after I arrived home with our first baby, my minister of music husband headed off to his office. I was left alone and wondering what I would do all day. I didn't know what to do or how to do it. What should I do first? I knew I had to nurse, dress, and snuggle my baby. Then the routine would start all over the next day…all day long…all week…all month.

I had just finished nursing our daughter when the doorbell rang. With her in my arms, I answered the door. To my surprise, there stood Mrs. Raymond Edwards. Before I could greet her, she announced, "I have come to be your mother!" My first thought was, "Does she know how to be my mother?"

Catching my breath, I managed to invite her in. She took her coat off and made herself comfortable in a chair close to me. My mind was racing!

What would she do? Was the house picked up and somewhat clean? Had I emptied that dirty diaper pail? Was our bed made? Were there dirty dishes in the sink?

She put me completely as ease. "Esther, I heard your mother could not come to be with you and every new mother needs her mother. So you relax and let me take care of you and Melody." With that statement, she took Melody in her arms and made over her…just like a mother would do. As she took Melody from my arms, I began to cry from her encouraging words to my heart.

My instinct was to offer her a cup of tea, but I did not even know how to make coffee. She said, "Esther, your job is to nurse and care for your baby and I am here to take care of you." She asked me to help her become familiar with the house. I did that, and then she left me to go draw bath water for Melody. She let me watch as she bathed my baby lovingly. After Melody was clean and dressed for the day, she showed me how to swaddle a baby. About that time, she insisted I get some rest, so I put Melody down and got back in bed. What an enormous gift this was! As I dozed off to sleep, I could hear the washing machine as it groaned under the load of diapers. When I awoke, it was noon, and she was there to serve me lunch. As I think back on those days, I do not remember if she brought food, or found something in the fridge. But it tasted very good!

After lunch, as we waited for Melody's next nursing time, we talked like mothers and daughters do. I learned so much from this godly mother and wonderful Bible teacher. I enjoyed "girl talk" with this woman I quickly came to trust with my heart. I loved the day with my new friend. I had no idea I would learn so much about life. Oh, I'd met her before, as her daughters were college classmates of mine, but now I was seeing her in a new light. I was getting the gift of an older, wiser woman pouring encouragement and hope into my life. She made me feel like I could do this important job of being a mom!

Late afternoon found us waiting for Bob to come home. When he walked through the back door, Mrs. Edwards walked out the front door as she explained that dinner was on the table, leaving our little family to a quiet evening. I was full of tears of gratitude for her gift of "mothering."

Imagine how surprised I was the next morning when she returned once again to gently care for mother and child. We talked more the next day. I cherished her wisdom and life experience.

When speaking to an audience of senior adults, I often say we *must* keep serving God, because only now do we have enough wisdom and life experience to pass on to another generation. This is exactly what my new friend was pouring into my life…an extraordinary gift.

Mrs. Edwards came every day for two weeks! I still weep as I think about this saint of God who ministered to a young minister's wife. May I pass on the baton of her gift to yet another young mother. It's a God Assignment. It is a legacy that must be passed on. And believe me, dear reader, young women desire this kind of relationship today.

Attention older women: Take note!

Attention younger women: Be bold and ask an older woman to be your prayer friend…exchanging legacies and impacting eternity!

Hope and Encouragement Hold Hands

We can exhibit hope in our homes, encouraging our children to believe God. One way you can do this is by telling your own personal faith stories.

Allow me to share an experience that helped me not to waver in my faith. In the mid-'70s, Melody and I made a trip to Germany to visit "like-family" friends. They were military people, and, when they picked us up at the airport and put our luggage in their car, they informed us that the car was a hand-me-down from another military couple and that it always needed *prayer coverage*. Truly, dear readers, it was held together by prayer and duct tape. So before we began our journey, we prayed. Late into the night, we pulled off the autobahn because of a deluge of rain and to pick up some bottled water for Molly, the mom, who was nursing a 6-week-old baby boy.

We got back in the car and Chris started the engine. As he did that, the car made a most awful sound. It was so loud that it woke the baby and my 16-year-old daughter. Lifting up the hood, Chris could see nothing because it was completely dark where we had parked. Sitting in the dark, I began to pray.

A young man came walking toward the car, and we discovered he spoke fluent German—while Chris spoke fluent English! Hand motions work...almost everywhere. The young man struck a match, held it over the engine, and found nothing. A second match...nothing. A third match...

found the problem. The car was fixed—using pliers and duct tape—and off we went. I am telling the truth here!

We still faced the dread of crossing the Austrian border —they have very strict car noise codes and our car was still making very strange car noises. Chris asked me to pray us through the border. Believe me, I hadn't stopped praying since we applied the duct tape to the engine. As we pulled away from the border, no one spoke. I began singing, through my tears, *"Praise God from Whom all blessings flow...."* Quickly, I was joined by our hosts and my daughter. We made it home safely in the wee hours of morning. It's one thing to be stranded in your own country. It is quite another for me to be stranded across the ocean... in another country...without my husband! What if I had never been taught to pray and sing the songs of faith? What would my hope have been in such a time as that? I don't want to trust my children and grandchildren to luck or happenstance; I want them to know the God Abraham trusted, *"being fully assured that what God had promised, He was able also to perform"* (Romans 4:21 NASB). Teach your

> *You and I are the matches . . . giving just enough light to guide our children and the generations to come, to be found faithful.*

children that God is able…in any home, city, state, or country.

Thinking back, I realized the young Swiss gentleman, who came out of nowhere to help, like an angel, gave us just enough light to take the next step. What encouragement! What hope!

You and I are the matches…giving just enough light to guide our children and the generations to come, to be found faithful.

Strike a match…
  …bless your world
    …read in your child's school
      …make time for family, often
        …volunteer in your child's church classes
          …start a neighborhood play group
            …read at local library story hour
              …help a new mother

Hope and encouragement hold hands.

Take the Courage out of Encouragement

Make a difference. Bless a child.

Mrs. Billy Graham does just this. I was in Black Mountain, North Carolina, a few years ago. I was visiting in one my favorite places, called *The Verandah*, which is a tea room and gift shop. The lady behind the counter was explaining to a customer that the needlework in her hand was the work of a non-profit, charitable corporation called *The Widow's Friend,* which works with Bangladesh widows in allowing them to keep their children from being sold or made slaves. These pieces of needlework are created by the poorest of the poor in Bangladesh. The art form is known as *nokshi kantha* or "quilted design." Such work is only done in Bangladesh. These gifted women take pride in their work and in the knowledge that they have a way to support their children.

I was all ears, listening in on this conversation. Looking around, I had spotted my life verse, Proverbs 3:5–6, in the quilted design art. I wanted to have it, for this verse has great meaning in my life, and perhaps my purchase would give meaning to a widow's life.

I looked at the price tag and seeing that it was quite high, quietly asked if there might be a smaller version. "No," she responded, "but I'm expecting Ruth (Graham) in here any day now and she will be bringing some new pieces. Ruth gets the work from *Widow's Friends.* She then pays out of her own pocket to have each one framed, and all the proceeds go to the Bangladesh women. We do not make any profit on these. Oh look! There she is now."

I turned and looked toward the door and in walked Mrs. Billy Graham (Ruth) and Gigi Tchividjian, her daughter. I mustered enough *courage* to introduce myself to Gigi. Her response surprised me! "Oh Esther! I know who you are! You spoke at my church last year, and I got your tapes. You are my sister Anne's friend, aren't you?" I nodded.

"Mother," she called to her mom, "come here and meet one of Anne's friends."

Ruth Graham is absolutely beautiful. I have never seen such clear blue eyes. She smiled at me and said, "Please excuse us. We have just come from the garden and I am not dressed for shopping." I thanked her for her work with the *Widow's Friend*. I shared with her the above conversation and my hesitancy because of the price of the needlework.

Taking hold of my arm, she said these words that pierced my heart: "Oh Esther! You *must* have that verse in your home. You will save the life of a child…you just must have it." Thanking her, off I went to make my purchase!

"Trust in the Lord with all your heart."
—Proverbs 3:5

It now proudly hangs in our family room and reminds me that He said, "…to the least of these, my little ones."

Thank you, Ruth Graham, for making a difference in my life. Walking out of the store with my then 10-year-old granddaughter, Anna Esther, she asked, "Nana, why are you crying?" "Anna, do you realize who that was? That was Ruth Graham, the wife of Dr. Billy Graham." "Nana, who is Dr. Billy Graham? Is he famous or something?"

Dear reader, do you see why we have to tell our stories to the next generation? It is not about us, but it is all about Him and His story in the lives of His children and how He engraves a life such as Dr. Billy Graham that will touch generations yet to be born. I am grateful for my friend,

Anne Graham Lotz, and pray daily for her as she teaches and encourages women all over the world. She is definitely leaving a legacy of faithful service to God, just like her father and her siblings.

Be sure your children are introduced to heroes of the faith, through books and personal encounters. It could be an "engraved" moment. Teach your children to live in God's hope, engraving life and leaving legacies.

Another keeper verse is 1 Thessalonians 5:11 (AMP):

> *"Therefore encourage [admonish, exhort] one another and edify [strengthen and build up] one another, just as you are doing."*

The story is told about a speaker at a women's retreat who suggested that the women ask their husbands to write a note and put it in their child's lunch box. What mother would not want that memory for her child? One woman took the suggestion seriously and asked her husband to write their young son. He agreed. Several weeks went by and the child had never mentioned receiving the notes. The father said to his wife, "This is not working! He has not one time mentioned my notes." "Please keep writing them," the mother begged. She reminded him that the speaker said this really works.

As mothers know, about six weeks into school there is that first PTA meeting. As the parents walked into their son's room and introduced themselves to the teacher, she immediately invited them to see their son's desk. As they approached the desk, the parents could see that the boy had taped every note his father had written to him to his desk! She said to the father, "You are not only blessing your son, sir. You are blessing every child in the class. Each day at lunch, the children gather around your son's desk as he reads your note. Thanks for your encouragement to this class."

Think back on your school days. Like me, I am sure you can name the teacher who first encouraged and challenged you. Remember how hard you worked to please that teacher or professor?

Everyone...needs encouragement.

Everyone...every day.

Everyone...all the days of our life!

Make it a *daily* practice to speak a word of encouragement to your child and watch them stand a bit taller, try just a bit harder, strive to reach higher, and you will see them begin to develop the habit of encouragement to others themselves. In this way, you are passing the baton. Remember: children imitate, copy, and tend to grow up to be like us! That's sometimes scary!

Give out large doses of encouragement—daily! Believe me, like a smile, encouragement given comes back as a gift. It is the gift of what it does to your heart and to the heart of the recipient. Encouragement is really the gift that keeps on giving. Encouragement builds esteem in our children. Yes, it is hard. I know it takes thought, but I also know it brings results. Children who live with daily encouragement will probably meet their goals. Children who live with constant criticism and little encouragement will struggle to live above the critical remarks.

Ms. Nickels was my fifth-grade teacher. Our class met in the attic, as best I remember, and we thought it was the greatest classroom in the school. Ms Nickels was a beautiful blonde, stylish in dress, and she smiled all the time. I was her favorite. No question about that. She let me put on class plays. I was trusted to run errands on her behalf, giving me *leadership status*. Was it her smile, her beauty, her gentleness, or her acceptance that encouraged a tall, gangly 5-foot, 7-inch fifth grader? It was all of the above! What a huge impact a teacher has on a child. A teacher's affirmation positively impacts a life. Pray with your children for their teachers. What a great gift this can be to both student and teacher.

Ms. Nickels encouraged me to believe in my gift of leadership. Did she have any idea she was touching a life that would be honored to touch other lives? Perhaps, she did.

Mr. Douglas, on the other hand, was my sixth-grade homeroom teacher, history teacher and...the school principal. He was feared. He walked the aisle with a ruler in his hand, always eager to swat the hand of an inattentive student. When teaching history, if he asked a question and the student could not give the correct answer, that student was sent to the back of the room. You stood there and could not return to your seat until you could correctly answer another question. I spent much of the sixth-grade history class standing at the back of the room! The effect of this teacher was indelible. I never got any encouragement in his class, except that my twin brother, David, a *brain*, would occasionally try to mouth the answer to me. I don't remember that it worked to my benefit. Needless to say, it was a painful year, and it was engraved on my memory for years. Then God reminded me that I was accepted and beloved, and invited me to take a seat in the front of the class. No more standing. Be careful with your words to your children. Words—positive or negative—have the power to engrave deep memories.

Encouraging Words Set Directions

Paul set a godly example for us in his encouragement to his spiritual son, Timothy. Paul speaks a word of encouragement to young Timothy, reminding him of his legacy in 2 Timothy 1:2:

> *"To Timothy, a beloved son: Grace, mercy, and peace from God the Father and Christ Jesus our Lord."*

What a lovely spiritual greeting from a father to his spiritual son. Consider writing that to your college child. What a blessing to be encouraged with the reminder of God's grace, mercy, and peace. Paul continues.

> *"I thank God, whom I serve with a pure conscience, as my forefathers did, as without ceasing*

I remember you in my prayers night and day, greatly desiring to see you, being mindful of your tears, that I may be filled with joy."

Add that last line to your child's letter. Paul recounts endearing memories of their shared tears together. Yes, it's true, parents. Our tears of joy and sorrow are remembered by our children and engraved on their hearts...forever.

"I call to remembrance the genuine faith that is in you, which dwelt first in your grandmother Lois and your mother Eunice, and I am persuaded is in you also."

Paul encourages Timothy with constant prayer.
   Paul writes how much he misses Timothy.
      Paul reminds Timothy of his spiritual legacy.
         Paul calls out Timothy's sincere faith.

At this time in Timothy's life, he may have been raised by a single mom. Have hope. A parent leaves a significant legacy. How gracious of God to give Timothy a "Paul." Ask that for your child as well. How these words must have given courage and hope to young Timothy...so much encouragement that Timothy became a biblical author alongside his spiritual father, Paul. Remember: the legacy you leave has the power to impact generations yet to be born!

Hope and Encouragement Hold Promises to Be Kept

Wouldn't you like to have seen the calendar that Jesus used to keep all the appointments with wannabes, relatives, tax collectors, fisherman, family men, doubters, deniers, blind and lame, down-and-outs, up-and-ins, tea party tree climbers, cripples, and the list goes on? What did he know about those He would call to himself? Of course, everything, and He knew what they would become...in Him. He knows the end from the beginning (Isaiah 46:10).

He knows the same about you and me—His precious daughters. What do you think God sees when He looks at you? What do you suppose He is writing about the future of your child? Could He be thinking—I need another...

...Billy Graham?
...Mother Teresa?
...D. L. Moody?
...Lottie Moon?
...C. S. Lewis?
...Beth Moore?

Each one...a kingdom changer!

Parents are human aids in a divine plan, part of God's master design that helps call another generation to obedience and Kingdom living. Look at God's track record with Kingdom changers who forever engraved Gods story:

- I don't think God saw Moses' stuttering tongue, but rather saw his ability to "turn aside" long enough to hear God's voice of instruction. God chose him to lead Israel out of slavery to the promised land.

- I don't think God saw Ruth as a Moabitess or outsider, but as the leading lady in the drama of redemption and His ancestor through King David.

- I don't think God saw Esther as a beauty queen, though He endowed her with beauty, but as a woman with the courage to advocate on behalf of His chosen people.

- I don't think Jesus saw Peter as a denier by the fire, but as the keynote speaker at Pentecost when the fire fell.

- I don't think Jesus saw Mary Magdalene as a demon-possessed woman, but as the last woman at the cross and first one at the grave...first to say "I have seen the Lord!"

- I don't think Jesus saw Paul as an enemy but as a tent-maker missionary. No wonder Jesus wanted Paul as an apostle. After all he had done to delete the truth of the gospel, God saw Paul become a Light to the Gentiles.

- I don't think that Jesus saw Rahab as a red-light lady, but rather as godly grandmother in His family tree, and a bearer of truth in the generations to come.

- I don't think God saw Lydia the entrepreneur as the CEO of Thyatira Dyed Fabrics, but as CEO (Chief Encouragement Officer) in the early church.

The list goes on and on. Want to add your favorites? Go ahead!

_____

_____

_____

_____

_____

_____

_____

_____

_____

Stop and meditate on your own life. Where do you find yourself in God's story today? Are you running strong with the faith baton? Will another generation know your God's story? Are you limping along, thinking it is not important? If so, you are wrong!

Create a Past for Your Children's Future

Think of it as a gift. Create ways to give the gift of a rich spiritual heritage to your children. Jesus did. He has given us every spiritual blessing...in Himself. We are blessed and we bless!

My heart longs for this generation to intentionally leave a spiritual legacy, a spiritual inheritance through their life story, and through God's story, touching generations yet to be born.

At the time I heard Dr. Charles Chaney tell this story, we were both serving together with the North American Mission Board. Dr. Chaney is a great storyteller. He caught my imagination with this story of a young Jewish boy who was part of the feeding of the five thousand. I loved how he embellished the story. I've added my own twist of imagination.

A young lad hears that the rabbi is coming to His community and he begs to go and see the teacher. Don't you just know his Jewish mother insisted he take along a lunch! He probably wasn't happy about it, but he was obedient, put it under his arm and off he went. The word on the street was that the teacher was coming from Bethsaida, and the crowds learned about it and followed him. He welcomed them and spoke to them about the kingdom of God and healed those who needed healing. Late in the afternoon, his disciples come to the teacher and said, "Master, send the crowd away so they can go to the surrounding villages and countryside and find food and lodging, because we are in a remote place." He replied, "You give them something to eat." They answered, "We have only five loaves of bread and two fish"...and you know the rest of the story.

But think about the young lad with the loaves and fishes. He is sitting by his buddy, maybe even hiding his lunch, when Andrew speaks up. *"Here is a boy with five small barley loaves and two small fish, but how far will they go among so many?"* (John 6:9 NIV). Andrew asked for the lad's lunch and after giving it, he immediately punches his buddy and with pride, says: "That's my lunch!" The lunch he did not want now has become *the* lunch. I can imagine he and his friend followed Andrew to the front row of the crowd. After all, remember he had *the lunch*. He delights as he watches what happened next!

> *"Jesus then took the loaves, gave thanks, and distributed to those who were seated as much as they wanted. He did the same with the fish. When they all had enough to eat, he said to his disciples, 'Gather the pieces that are left over. Let nothing be wasted.'"*
>
> —John 6:11–12 (NIV)

I can imagine the young boy's eyes as he watches this miracle happen…and he quietly punches his buddy and whispers, "That's…not my lunch!"

Encouragement is like that. So are legacies. We receive it and pass it along. It is not ours to keep. *"Every good and every perfect gift is from above, and comes down from the Father of lights"* (James 1:17) These good and perfect gifts can be a legacy to your child and grandchild. Keep passing the baton. Never stop! Keep…on…passing…the…baton!

Legacies
ᴏꜰ HOPE AND LOVE

- Give children/grandchildren a yearly Christmas ornament.
- Have child's photo made into a puzzle.
- Make up a play about your family. Dress up and put on a show.
- Create a birthday scrapbook for each child…add yearly school photos.
- Dad's night out with child.
- Plan a family evening.
  Make this a regular occurrence.
  Turn off the TV and telephone.
  Pick the dates and write them in the family calendar.
  Remind the family about the upcoming game night.
  Check that the board games are complete.
  Plan a simple supper.
  Decide on which game to play, or let the kids pick the game.
  Everyone plays.
  Expect easy laughs and good fun! You are building legacies!
- End the night with each family member speaking a blessing to every other family member.

Legacies of Written and Spoken Words

I recently updated my cell phone. My new one can do so much more than I am interested in doing! While visiting family for Christmas, Granddaughter Anna Esther, age 15, showed me all the bells and whistles on my phone. Heading home in the car, I thought, "I'll just spend some time in the guidebook and maybe learn more about it." Opening my new phone, I discovered these words written on the screen:

I love U Nana! U are the best. AER
(Anna Esther Reid)

I'm smiling! Now that's a "written word" I'll not erase. Want to know what I like about written notes? You can read them over and over and over again.

I recently spent an afternoon "down memory lane" in preparation for this chapter, reading letters from my letter box from my children, my husband, parents, and friends. I had to finally stop as the tears and laughter filled my lap. These are indeed treasured memories. I spent part of the day embraced with family moments, crises, vacations, graduations, weddings, legacies from childhood homes, and 48 years of being the *Burroughs Family*. Words are truly a gift!

God's Words...About God's Word

> "For the mouth speaks out of that which fills the heart. The good man brings out of his good treasure what is good; and the evil man brings out of his evil treasure what is evil."
>
> —Matthew 12:34*b*–35 (NASB)

I like the way New International Version states verse 35:

> "For out of the overflow of the heart the mouth speaks. The good man brings good things out of

the good stored up in him, and the evil man brings evil things out of the evil stored up in him."

I love the word "overflow." Webster says it means: 1. "to flow across; flood" 2. "to flow over the brim of." That says it, does it not? I think that is what Jesus is saying; the overflow flows over the brim, impacting our lives!

Listen to the Amplified Bible translation:

"For out of the fullness (the overflow, the superabundance) of the heart the mouth speaks. The good man from his inner good treasure flings forth good things, and the evil man out of his inner evil storehouse flings forth evil things."

God's Word is so clear about our words. No wonder Paul reminds us in Philippians 4:7 (NASB):

"And the peace of God, which surpasses all comprehension, will guard your hearts and your minds in Christ Jesus."

We will need His peace in our hearts and minds, helping us to focus on engraving our spoken and written words in and to our families.

Words Matter!

In an instant—a heartbeat—words can alter lives, completely change circumstances, give life, and deal death-blows. Words curse and bless, and all from the same mouth. I wish this were not so. Proverbs 18:21 (NIV) teaches:

> *"The tongue has the power of life and death, and those who love it will eat its fruit."*

If we speak *words of life,* we will enjoy the life-giving fruit. If we speak words of death, we experience words of death. James warns us sternly in James 3:8–10 (AMP):

> *"But the human tongue can be tamed by no man. It is a restless [undisciplined, irreconcilable] evil, full of deadly poison. With it we bless the Lord and Father, and with it we curse men who were made in God's likeness! Out of the same mouth come forth blessing and cursing. These things, my brethren, ought not to be so."*

This is a breathtaking truth. Stop! Take in—absorb—listen to this message. We bless those made in the image of God, or we curse those made in the image of God. I'm thinking: "How dare we?" But I'm sure I have done both. And like you, I feel and know the difference in my innermost being, when I speak a word—I have blessed or cursed. Give praise for the Holy Spirit, our Teacher whispers: *"That was not My spirit in your words,"* or *"Yes, My spirit was in your words."*

Listen to Paul's warning in Colossians 4:6:

"Let your speech always be with grace, as though seasoned with salt, so that you will know how you should respond to each person."

Remember this about salt...it
    preserves
        enhances
            flavors
                heals

How tasty our words would be if we consistently seasoned them with grace. Try this experiment for 30 days: Before you speak, imagine how your words will taste to those who will hear them. Ask the father to season your words with *grace*.

If this works for you and you can tell a difference, get your children to join you for another 30 days and see what will happen in your home. Engrave in your child's mind how to speak *grace words* in the most important place on earth...the home.

In 1 Peter 3:15, the Amplified Bible expresses it this way:

"But in your hearts set Christ apart as holy [and acknowledge Him] as Lord. Always be ready to

give a logical defense to anyone who asks you to account for the hope that is in you, but do it courteously and respectfully."

I think this encouragement is about hourly, moment-by-moment, daily living and not just an occasion when we are sharing Christ. We are *resurrection people*, living as kingdom bearers—bearing the good news, full of hope and courage, because Christ lives in us, seasoning us with grace.

Words Unfitly Spoken

It was a privilege for Bob and me to attend our son's college senior composition recital at the University of South Carolina. We made the three-and-a-half-hour drive from Atlanta to Columbia and had such a fun evening! We had every right to be proud parents. We had a very special gift for our son and promised to take him and his friends out to dinner after the recital. We presented the gift of two wooden batons. One baton was carved out of wood from the log cabin home of the great Baptist hymn writer B.B. McKinney. The other was the rehearsal baton of Bob's college mentor/teacher from Oklahoma Baptist University, Dean Warren M. Angell. I framed the batons with brass name plates, identifying each one. It was a special event together, and, in a real sense, it was the passing of the baton from one generation to another.

As we started home after dinner, Bob said, "Now, babe, you are going to have to stay awake and help me make this trip back to Atlanta." I much prefer sleeping in the car late at night, you understand, but I said, "I can do that if you will stop and get me McDonald's coffee and cookies."

Knowing my man's driving patterns, I said, "I will start looking for the next McDonald's." I sat close to the windshield, and it was not long until I spied the famous golden arches. "There it is," I said as I pointed. *Swish*! Right on past we drove as quick as a flash. Folding my arms in disgust, I said, "What's the matter? Didn't you see it?" He responds: "We'll get the next one." I know better. The man is like a horse heading to the barn. There is no stopping him.

Understand his mind. We just can't let another car get ahead of us.

Arms still folded, looking determined, and sitting even closer to the windshield, I said, "I'll find the next one." I was ready. "See it," I yelled? Off I-20 he goes. At the light, wouldn't you know it? McDonald's was on the opposite side of the highway, so Bob pulls into Hardees instead. "What was that you wanted?" he asks me as he begins to talk into the order box. "That would be McDonald's coffee and McDonald's cookies!" I respond. "This won't do?" I'm thinking anybody knows you can't get McDonald's coffee and McDonald's cookies at Hardees! "Forget it!" he says into the speaker and he tears, yes, tears out of Hardees, pulls across the road and into the McDonald's drive-through and orders exactly what I'd asked for 40 minutes earlier. He ordered nothing for himself. I didn't care. I'd have my picnic all by myself. I didn't even share a cookie. For the next hours, he cleared his throat...*harrumph*...in a low register and I responded by clearing my throat...*harrumph*...in a high register.

Are you just dying laughing at us? Because I know you have had this "throat-clearing conversation" with someone in your life, maybe even recently!

In silence, except for an occasional *harrumph*, we stayed wide awake. Ever notice how the Evil One trips us up after we have experienced a Holy moment? And it was all over a cup of coffee! But you understand? It wasn't my fault. I'd stated my expectations!

Notice the little word, "*my.*" It gets me every time as I use that word too much. This clearing-our-throat conversation ended the next morning with written and spoken words.

I was taking a graduate class at Georgia State in, of all things, "Marriage and Family." I know what you're thinking. "*She sure needs that class,*" and you'd be right. Getting in the car early the next morning, headed to school, I noticed a yellow sticky note on the steering wheel. Attached to the sticky note was a dollar bill. The note said: "Here is your McDollar for your McDonald's coffee on your way to McGraduate class.*" I was certain this was his apology. After all, it was his fault! (I hope you are laughing.) I ran upstairs, put my arms round him, and asked his forgiveness. We had wasted hours of pleasant company over a cup of coffee. He forgave me and I him.

Only recently, while driving me to a speaking engagement, Bob quietly said, "I never tire of your company.

I enjoy these times with you. I'd rather be in your company than anyplace I know." "Thanks, I feel the same way," I said. Whew! Sometimes we get the right seasoning in our words.

Written Words

Christmas 2003 was a Burroughs Christmas. I had a happy-happy mother and grandmother heart as all the family gathered under our roof. My favorite gift that year was a book titled *Why I Love Grandma*. Each page gives a statement. Here's one: "I love Grandma because…her faith in me gives me confidence."

My granddaughters had written on certain pages how they felt about the statement on the page about grand-mothers. One of my grandchildren wrote: "She is the most mature Christian I know. I learn new things from her all the time."

Another page reads: "I love my Grandma because she sends me cards to remind me that she loves me, and sends Bible verses to remind me that God does, too."

Bob went to the trouble of sending the book to our children so the grandchildren could write on any page they chose ahead of time. Yes, I wept.

Hurry! Put this book down and call your local bookstore or go online and purchase this book. But hurry back! I will be counting on you to finish my book. Plan a special time with your children to write notes to their grandparents on the pages of this book before you give it to them. It will be their favorite present. The book is all about legacies and memories we make in the shelter of family. Why? We all need encouragement, and coming from a grandparent, this becomes an engraved treasure for any grandchild.

Words Engraved for a Lifetime

Today is January 6, 2005. I was directed this morning in my devotions to 1 Thessalonians 4:16*a*: *"For the Lord Himself will descend from heaven with a shout"* (NASB). But I saw 5:11 underlined, so I read it also: *"Therefore encourage one another and build up one another, just as you also are doing"* (NASB). On another day, I'd written Galatians 5:15 in the margin. So off I went to Galatians 5:15: *"but if you bite and devour one another, take care that you are not consumed by one another"* (NASB).

I looked again at the words "build up" and that led me to Ephesians 4:29: *"Let no unwholesome word proceed from your mouth, but only such as is good for edification according to the need of the moment, so that it will give grace to those who hear"* (NASB).

Wow! What a great family verse to pray for and with your family this year! Let me encourage you to find a Scripture to pray for your family this year and a new one each year. Your family will likely memorize it as it is prayed often around your table, thus engraving His words in the life of your children.

In my early childhood, I heard words like "Pretty is as pretty does" "Beauty is only skin deep," and "Be a lady." I seldom heard words of affirmation, such as "Well done," "We are proud of you," or "I love you." Sadly, it was the way of that generation and many of them never heard their parents express love. Yes, they took care of essential needs and this was their "love language."

How they would have bene-fited from Gary Chapman's book, *The Five Love Languages of Children* (a great book for couples and parents). All chil-dren in my generation were treated just the same. But I can tell you this: My grandfather Milligan had a special name for me. I can still see him, on the farm in his sittin' place (which was a metal tractor seat nailed to tree stump) smoking his pipe and curling up his mustache. He would gather me onto his lap, and snuggle me, calling me "Wee Essie." I had a great Aunt Esther, whom the family called "Essie." I never met her, but it pleased my granddaddy to call me his little one. Words like that fill a child's heart, lift the spirit, and fill the longing for "home."

Let me encourage you to find a Scripture to pray for your family this year and a new one each year.

Every child needs to hear positive words, and most espe-cially words from those who love them. I feel that words touch like hugs touch. Words tear like barbwire tears.

Words heal like soothing rain. In fact, words engraved in our hearts at any moment or experience can come back to warm us—or continue to hurt us.

Visiting in our daughter's home, I walked into the family room just in time to catch some endearing words between Bob, whom the grandkids called "Bop," and Anna, our first grandchild. They were both on the floor coloring to their hearts content. I heard him say, "Anna, I wasn't a real good dad, but I'm gonna be a real good granddaddy." "OK," she said. Little did she know how true that would be. Ask her about her Bop! Be encouraged. I think fathers tend to mellow and make wonderful grandfathers.

Finally, I learned to ask for an expression of love from my parents. My mother's habit was, when talking to me, to brag on all my brothers and sisters, keeping me updated from their letters and calls. She seldom asked about me. And when my mom talked to my brothers, she told them all about me and what I was doing! At least, in this manner, I received their affirmation, but I just did not want it second-hand. I finally got the courage to ask my parents to just tell me they were proud and that they loved me, and, thankfully, they began to do so.

Don't make your children have to ask you if they are loved. It's their heritage in a Christian home and they deserve your love. If your mother didn't do it, you do it! Break that cycle. God is pleased when we encourage and affirm our children. Make it a God-stop…engraving a child's heart!

In the early '70s, I was invited to Oklahoma University to attend a summer meeting for campus ministers who served our denominational universities. I checked the family calendar and we decided that professionally, this was something I needed to do. In preparation for my week away from my second-grade son and fifth-grade daughter as well as my college professor husband, I prepared spaghetti, chicken casserole, meat loaf, pound cake, and lots of surprises. Each was packed away in the freezer, labeled with complete cooking instructions. I felt like they would be fine with the meals in my absence.

Early Sunday morning, I parked my car at Samford University and met the van and eight other campus ministers. After 13 long hours in the van, we arrived on the OU campus. My roommate for the week was a former missionary who was now working with college students. She was up at the crack of dawn (well, really before it cracked), and she was on her knees conversing with God. My, how well she knew Him. I came to bless God that she met Him so early. Little did I know how I would need her prayers. But I am getting ahead of myself!

I found a hall phone booth and placed a collect call home. This, of course, was way before the days of cell phones. My husband Bob answered.

"We're here safe and settled in the dorm. How was your day?" I asked. Long pause.

"Well, to start with, David got sick on the church bus at day camp. They called for me to come get him, help clean up the bus, and take him home."

"Oh my! Is he OK now? I can get on a plane and come home!" I said.

"No, I'm doing fine. I can handle it. But what day is it that you are coming home?"

"Saturday night, but really I can get home."

"No, I can manage."

"Is everything else OK?" I inquired.

"Well. Actually, Melody was jumping on the trampoline at the neighbors' house, fell, and dislocated her arm. So I've spent the afternoon in the emergency room with her."

I groaned and insisted that I return home.

"No, I can handle this. It's quiet right now, but you are coming home on Saturday, right?"

Don't make your children have to ask you if they are loved. It's their heritage in a Christian home and they deserve your love.

"Right! And please tell me nothing else has happened in the last 12 hours?"

Long pause. "Well, you will want to know that Tabitha the cat has given birth to five kittens…*under our bed*," he emphasized.

"Let me call Delta and get home."

"No, I can handle this, but you hurry home Saturday."

Believe me, I was ready to hurry home Saturday. I was so happy to drive onto the Samford campus, get in my car, and head home. Turning left from Highway 280 onto

Overton Road, I noticed what looked like a garage sale sign painted by kids. I missed the wording and kept driving. About a fourth of a mile on down the road, I noticed another sign, same paint color and same printing. I took notice of this one.

Welcome Home, Mom! Yea! Home cooking tonight!!

I smiled. That might be my children! Not certain, I drove on and quickly came to another sign.

Esther Mom comes home today!

What an engraved message for my heart. All the way home about every fourth of a mile, another sign was posted. As I turned into the driveway, honking the horn, announcing my arrival, I noticed a huge sing engraved with these words:

In sickness or in health, the world's greatest mom is home today!

Gales of laughter, hugs, and kisses were shared all over that driveway. The children could not wait for me to come into the house. The kitchen table was set, name cards were at each place, my chair decorated with still more love signs. Dinner was prepared. Gifts were on my plate. My heart was full. I insisted we take a break to go outside and take a photo of the sign and the kids. I wanted proof that they called me the world's greatest mom! I knew the teen days were not far off, and felt sure that some day they might not agree with what the sign said. For a week or so, I had so much fun at the grocery store as I overheard women talking about the signs along Overton Road.

"Wonder who 'Esther' is?"

"Wonder how long she had been gone?"

"How fortunate she is to have her family welcome her home in such a way!"

I smiled, never admitting I was that lucky mother. This was a scrapbook memory for sure.

As important as my children's words were to me that afternoon, that was not the first encouraging words I'd been given. Isaiah the prophet says in Isaiah 49:8 (NASB):

> *"Thus says the Lord, 'In a favorable time I have answered you,*
> *And in a day of salvation I have helped you;*
> *and I will keep you and give you for a covenant of the people,*
> *To restore the land, to make them inherit the desolate heritages.'"*

Picking up at verse 13:

> *"Shout for joy, O heavens! And rejoice, O earth.*
> *Break forth into joyful shouting, O mountains!*
> *For the Lord has comforted His people,*
> *And will have compassion on His afflicted.*
> *But Zion said, 'The Lord has forsaken me, and the Lord has forgotten me.'"*

The Lord answers in verse 15:

"Can a woman forget her nursing child, and have no compassion on the son of her womb? Even these may forget, but I will not forget you. Behold I have inscribed you on the palms of My hands; Your walls are continually before Me."

Now that is an engraving—a permanent engraving! Both of His hands bear the name, *Esther*, the world's greatest daughter! He bears your name, too, dear reader!

Create a Past for Your Children's Future

What road signs or mileposts are you placing in the lives of your children today that will become *engraved memories?* How are you passing the baton of encouragement to your family, making lasting legacies and hope for generations yet to be born? Teach your children to look for ways to encourage a friend, neighbor, or family member. Make it a game! They will surprise you and it will become a habit.

Bob and I are creating a past for our grandtwins, Milligan and Walker, today. We are using two wonderful books. I take them to piano lessons, and of course we have snacks on the way—it's a Nana job! Bob, when he is finished teaching his class, picks them up and brings them to our home. When Walker gets out of the car, he says, "Nana, let's do the words first!" After "the words," we do crafts and games. We are big on activities with grandchildren because that's making memories. It's our job. We are creating a past for our grandchildren's future today. What we do with our children today, they will, in future days, remember and cherish the legacy. Parents, this is true for you, also. Please make time for fun family activities. Don't leave that up to after-school programs. As good as they are, it is not family playing, creating, and working together.

The books we use are: *God's Wisdom for Little Boys* and *God's Wisdom for Little Girls* by Jim and Elizabeth George. These books are full of character-building fun from the Bible book of Proverbs. The colorful paintings are beautiful. Each page names a characteristic, has a four-line poem, and has a Proverbs Scripture. Bob reads to Walker, and I read to Milligan. Then we get the crayons, kept in their craft drawer, and go to the kitchen table. Each child has a page with his or her name at the top. They copy the word we read that day then post their pages on the bulletin board in the kitchen. Our game is this: when we catch them "being" one of the characteristics, they get to place a star by that word—words like helpful, wise, kind, cheerful, diligent, friendly, and thrifty. We feel we are supporting their parents in helping the children learn godly habits. When we finish these books, we will do them a second time. It takes time to build character. Eventually, the twins will get to keep these books.

In her book *Edges of His Ways*, Amy Carmichael tells this story:

> *"Dr. F.B. Meyer once told me that when he was young, he was very irritable, and an old man*

told him that he had found relief from this very
thing by looking up the moment he felt it coming,
and saying. 'Thy sweetness, Lord.' By telling this,
that old man greatly helped Dr. Meyer, and he
told it to tens of thousands of people. I pass it on
to you because I have found it a certain and
quick way of escape. Take the opposite of your
temptation and look up inwardly, naming that
opposition:

Untruth—Thy truth, Lord;
Unkindness—Thy kindness, Lord;
Impatience—Thy patience, Lord;
Selfishness—Thine unselfishness, Lord;
Roughness—Thy gentleness, Lord;
Dishonesty—Thy courtesy, Lord;
Resentment, inward heat, fuss—Thy sweetness,
Lord, Thy calmness, Thy peacefulness. I think
that no one who tries this very simple plan will
ever give it up. It takes for granted, of course, that
all is yielded and 'I' is dethroned. Will all to
whom this is new, please try it for a day, a week,
a month and test it?"

Perhaps this is a story for a parent to experience and practice. Your family will see and taste your gracious words. But I also think this can be a teaching story to help your child handle life's circumstances.

Written Words Become Spoken Words...
—As the Reader Hears the Writer's Voice

I was 40 years old when the words of my father deeply engraved my life. I have every hand-written or typed letter my parents ever sent me. One thing was constant in their writing: Every letter ended with a verse of Scripture and, most often, this statement from my Father: "Keep looking up. Jesus sits at the right hand of the Father."

When I received a birthday card on my 40th birthday, I knew there would be a Scripture reference under my parent's signature. By the way, parents—this idea can become a legacy between you and your children, whether written by hand or sent by email. I had many cards to open that day, so I did not take the time to check out the Scripture reference. I stuck the card in a book and was delighted several months later when it reappeared since I had forgotten about it. I read the card again, savoring each word, and then I looked at the Scripture they had given me:

> *"Strength and honor are her clothing;*
> *She shall rejoice in time to come.*
> *She opens her mouth with wisdom,*
> *And on her tongue is the law of kindness.*
> *She watches over the ways of her household,*
> *And does not eat the bread of idleness.*
> *Her children rise up and call her blessed;*
> *Her husband also, and he praises her:*
> *Many daughters have done well,*

But you excel them all.
Charm is deceitful and beauty is passing,
But a woman who fears the Lord, she shall be
*   praised."*

—Proverbs 31:25–30

Yes, I wept and wept. Any daughter would weep if her father sent these precious words to her. I felt like my father was giving me a blessing as his daughter. I had longed for his verbal blessing all my childhood.

My father's words to me always included a word from God's Word for my life; it was indeed a double-engraved treasure. His *written* words became *spoken* words to my heart as I could picture in my mind my father speaking this Scripture to me. You just have to love that he included verse 29, bragging on me through God's words as well as reminding me charm is deceitful and beauty is passing! How well I know, as I get older!

Words are pictures through which we feel life. Pictures were engraved in our memories and stored in our hearts long before the advent of digital cameras. Words often can't be forgotten. In gladness, that's a pleasant thing. In sadness, it's a hard thing. Words, like pictures, can leave deeply engraved images on a child's heart. Have you heard yourself saying statements like these:

"The last thing she said to me was...."
"You always...."

"His words touched me deeply. I could see what he was saying…."

"You never…."

"Remember what Mother always said…."

Reckless words pierce like a sword, but the tongue of the wise brings healing. Often, our words hurt the very people we love the most. Criticism can destroy the self-worth of family members and create an atmosphere of distrust. Encouraging words also impact relationships, lifting our spirits, enhancing our self-esteem, engraving an image on our minds and hearts, and positively impacting our lives.

I remember a time when my children were so unkind to each other. We started a "positive word" game. If I heard a put-down of their sibling, they had to add a kind word after the not-so-kind word. Of course it made us laugh and get over the insult. It also made us think before we spoke damaging words. Remember, parents, positive words after negative words; it softens the blow and may change habits. You could of course attach an award to this habit. Give it a try for two weeks and see if there is improvement among siblings.

Words That Make a Difference!

Thank you. These two words are essential in any and all relationships. These words should be used often in family—given by parents' example and then copied by children. It is good for our hearts to express gratitude. Children need to learn this word very early in life. When our grandtwins were babies, they said *please* and *thank you* with sign language. Gratitude is a gift you give to yourself as well as to others. It brings to us a sense of grace, making us grateful.

Writing notes of gratitude and thanks is another lesson children should learn early. I know some parents who will not allow their children to play with birthday toys until the thank-you note is written! My husband is the world's best thank-you note writer. I've watched through his years of ministry as he would write encouraging and thank-you notes to a wide variety of people. Expressing thanks and appreciation through written or spoken words is a reflection of inner gratitude, and it is not about seasonal expressions, but daily expressions. Gratitude is a godly characteristic and much needed in our world. Certainly the psalms are full of grateful expressions. Another idea for parents: with the help of a good concordance, look up the word *thank(s)* in the Bible and begin reading a verse each day at the breakfast table that expresses thanks and gratitude. Consider naming a day of the week as *Official Thank-you Day* and see how many times your family members can genuinely express thanks and appreciation to each other and others. At the dinner table, allow each one to share the responses received when saying thank you. This could become a monthly tradition.

I'm sorry. Using these two words can change family situations drastically. Recently, after speaking to a women's ministry group, a lady put this note in my hand:

"Be what you is and not what you ain't
For if you ain't what you is,
Then you is what you ain't."

Isn't it true that often when we have to say *I'm sorry*, it is because *"we is what we ain't?"* That makes me think of hearing Chuck Swindoll on his radio program many years ago telling about a friend building his children a tree house. When completed, the children put a sign on the tree house door that read:

"Nobody act big!
　　Nobody act small!
　　　　Everybody act medium!"

Now wouldn't family life be easier if everyone acted *medium?* It seems to me that we act *big* when we feel *small*, and we act *small* when our actions should be based on who we are in Christ—who knit us together in our mother's womb.

The Amplified Bible says in Psalms 139:14*b*–15:

"Wonderful are Your works, and that my inner self knows right well. My frame was not hidden from You when I was being formed in secret [and] intricately and curiously wrought [as if embroidered with various colors] in the depths of the earth."

Wrought is a word used by artists, painters, and sculptors as they sign their works of creation. Needlework and embroidery in past generations were signed *"wrought by"* followed by the artist's name. We are God's signature piece as if embroidered in various colors. As parents, we are to celebrate the various colors of each child, celebrating their DNA, knowing the Divine Artist's gift in creating life and blessing it.

Help your child act *medium*, being their best self. Often in family, we will have to say, *"I'm sorry."* We live under the same roof, with the same people, trying not to act *big* or *small* but rather acting as *medium* people, knowing how to say:

"Please forgive me."

"I am sorry."

And we learn to move on. Forgiveness makes way for grace-living and it is all part of growing and accepting ourselves and helping our children accept themselves by acknowledging their godly characteristics, thus helping them know how to act *medium*. Being yourself is a *gift* to you and your family.

I love you. Is there any more important words spoken than these three words? They clothe all other words, allowing forgiveness, encouragement, thankfulness, and kindness, just to name a few. We are reminded about loving in 1 Peter 4:8, 10 (NASB):

> *"Above all, keep fervent in your love for one another, because love covers a multitude of*

sins...As each one has received a special gift, employ it in serving one another as good stewards of the manifold grace of God."

Our families need this kind of love. We need the many-folded grace of God covering us, as we cover our families and the multitudes of...

dirty towels
attitudes
messy rooms
bad habits
mistakes

Think of your love as a pleated skirt with many folds, covering your child—never-ending folds of God's love through your love. Hard work? Yes. You are engraving another generation that will teach generations to come. It is worth it!

I was speaking at New Orleans Baptist Seminary several years ago. I was invited to the home of then-President Leavell for dessert after the evening session. There is not a more gracious lady than his wife, JoAnn Leavell! I was sitting near Dr. Landrum Leavell in the family room when the phone rang. I heard Dr. Leavell say, "Hi son! It is so good to hear your voice. How was the game? You scored? Great! You won? Thanks for calling, son. I am so proud of you, I love you."

I was thinking: What a fortunate college student to be told he is loved, by his father. These were indeed words of grace, engraved on a child's heart, never to be deleted, always to be cherished.

Fathers: Your children never get tired of hearing you express your love to them. Even when they don't like you, asking you to drop them off a block from school, they still want to hear you say you love them. Say it often. The words *I love you*, expressed as grace words, become a legacy gift.

Be Kind. When my Reid grandgirls were small, I was teaching them Ephesians 4:32, which says: "Be kind one to another." When their dad came home, of course, I wanted them to show off. They got their dad's attention and began: "Be kind one (long pause) …two…three." I would observe that our homes need kindness one…two…three… hundreds of times daily, don't you agree?

Kindness truly works. If it does not change the other person, it will change you—the very reason to act in kindness. The apostle Paul gives us great words for godly family characteristics. In Colossians chapter three, he encourages us to put on the *new self*. Then, he tells us what to take off… *"anger, wrath, malice, slander and abusive speech from our mouth"* (Colossians 3:8 NASB) (kindness will help us here). Next, in Colossians 3:12–13 (NASB), Paul tells us what to put on:

> *"So, as those who have been chosen of God, holy and beloved, put on a heart of compassion, kindness, humility, gentleness and patience; bearing with one another* [This means acting 'medium,' don't you think?] *and forgiving each other."*

This passage would make a wonderful family night reading and discussion.

During Nana's Summer Camp 2004, we followed an Olympics theme and our motto was: "*Go for the Gold. Run with the Son.*" We did everything by teams, except our Bible study, which was led by my son David. He did a study on 1 Corinthians 13:4–8, which was a great study for any family gathered at the beach for seven days—in the same house, at the same table, in the same pool, on the same beach! Know what I mean? At the end of the study, he led us in a very thought-provoking exercise that helped us see our "love quotient." He invited us to truthfully put our name in the place of the word *love*. For example, *Nana is patient, Nana is kind* and so on. Try it. You might make this idea a family altar exercise helping your family members discover their love quotient. It occurs to me this might be a good New Year's family event...and check it again in six months to encourage growth in Christ. It's not difficult. But it is thought-provoking and challenging.

As a child, David was teaching our family about *kindness.* One New Year's Eve, our family sat together and wrote out our individual and family goals. David wrote on his page: *Act like guests.* I asked, "Son, do you mean you want us to be like guests?" He replied: "No, I want us to talk to each other like we talk to our guests." Ouch! Acting *medium* could make that happen, don't you think?

In Amy Carmichael's book *Edges of his Ways,* she writes a devotion for August 8 entitled, *The Three Sieves.* A sieve is a bowl with holes in it used to strain water from food. It separates the needed from the not-needed. Here are the three:

> *"1. Is it true?*
> *2. Is it kind?*
> *3. Is it necessary?*
>
> *All of us who have tried to remember and use these three sieves know what a help they can be. We are sorry when we forget them, and we are very grateful when we are reminded of them in time to keep us from saying something untrue, unkind, or unnecessary! Perhaps these three sieves will help to keep some words from being spoken that would grieve the spirit of love and hurt someone whom our Lord loves."*

Is it true? Is it kind? Is it necessary?

Let me confess to you, dear reader, her words convicted my heart, or is it my tongue? Wounding someone with our words deeply grieves the Spirit of love—when we do, we hurt someone who God loves. Let that sink in.

One last word from the Word. Jesus began His public ministry teaching in the Temple:

> *"And He began to say to them, 'Today this Scripture has been fulfilled in your hearing.'*

*And all were speaking well of Him, and wonder-
ing at the gracious words which were falling
from His lips; and they were saying, 'Is this not
Joseph's son?'"* (Luke 4:21–22 NASB)

My prayer for you and me is that we will speak well of Him
in our families and they will be amazed at the *gracious
words* falling from our lips, leaving a legacy of words well
spoken.

Legacies

～ OF WRITTEN AND SPOKEN WORDS

- Bless your children today with encouraging words, both spoken and written.

- Make Monday "Speak Kindly to Family Day"—all day.

- On car trips, make up stories using words that begin with all of the alphabet letters, in order.

- Put sticky love notes on bathroom mirrors.

- Make "Fun Zone" or "Quiet Zone" signs to be used by family members, as needed.

- Make thank-you cards a family event for any occasion.

- Write love notes to great-aunts/uncles and great-grandparents.

- Check out of your library such great books as *Letters to Philip* and *Letters to Karen* by Charlie Shedd.

- Place handwritten notes to family members on your Christmas tree.

Resources

1. *Why I Love Grandma: 100 Reasons* by Gregory E. Lang and Meagan Lang, published by Cumberland House Publishing Inc.

2. *Edges of his Ways: Selections for Daily Reading* by Amy Carmichael, published by Christian Literature Crusade

3. *God's Wisdom for Little Boys* by Jim and Elizabeth George, published by Harvest House Publishers

4. *God's Wisdom for Little Girls* by Jim and Elizabeth George, published by Harvest House Publishers

Legacies of Prayer

"The prayer of the heart is the prayer of intimacy. It is the prayer of love and tenderness of a child to Father God. Like a mother hen, who gathers her chicks under her wings, we, through the prayer of the heart, allow God to gather us to himself—to hold us, to coddle us, to love us."

—Richard Foster, *Prayer: Finding the Heart's True Home*

*D*on't you love the thought of Abba Father gathering us to Himself as illustrated by the image of a mother gathering her brood, like a hen gathers her chicks? Another Scripture image speaks of God's "parent heart" and His longing for His children. Matthew 23:37 (*The Message*) says: *"Jerusalem! Jerusalem!... How often I've ached to embrace your children...and you wouldn't let me."* The Amplified Bible says: *"you refused!"*

Please believe that God desires to love us just like that. Have you ever tried to hug and kiss a child who would not let you? That hurts. Our heavenly Father continually invites you and me to "come home." He stands with outstretched arms to welcome us to His presence. Richard Foster, in his book *Prayer: Finding the Heart's True Home*, says it like this:

> *"He invites us into the living room of his heart, where we can put on old slippers, and share freely. He invites us into the kitchen of his friendship, where we chatter and batter mix in good fun. He invites us into the dining room of his strength, where we can feast to our heart's delight. He invites us into the study of his wisdom, where we can learn and grow and stretch...and ask all the questions we want. He invites us into the workshop of his creativity, where we can be co-laborers with him, working together to determine the outcomes of events. He invites us into the bedroom of his rest, where new peace is found and where we can be naked and vulnerable and free. It is also the place of deepest intimacy where we know and are known to the fullest.*

The key to this home, this heart of God, is prayer. If the key is prayer, the door is Jesus Christ."

Invited by the King to the Throne Room

It was early morning in my childhood home. I quietly left my bedroom, crossing the hallway to the bathroom to begin making my preparations for the day. I heard my father's familiar voice. *Who could he be talking to this early in the morning?* I pondered. Like any inquisitive child, I followed the sound of his voice. The door stood slightly ajar—and I carefully peeked inside. I have carried this Kodak moment all of my life. My preacher-daddy was on his knees, Bible open on his chair, and he was tenderly praying the Psalms back to God. I felt a hushed presence. I knew my daddy knew to whom he was talking! It was so obvious. He was so intimately acquainted with his heavenly Father.

Even as a child, I wanted to know God like that. I stood there, sort of hoping that *presence* would get on me. In the ensuing years, I have discovered I can know God like that—by meeting God like that—daily. My precious daddy taught me by example to practice the presence of Christ. *Prayer* is a conversation that never ends. That should thrill women, because we are relational, and in *this* conversation, the listener, the friend *never stops listening/talking.*

I am so glad my father's study door was open that morning. I am so glad my heavenly Father's door is always open.

God Invites Us to Use His Name

This is a powerful truth: When we pray, God invites us to use His name. John 14:13–14 (NIV) says: *"I will do whatever you ask in my name, so that the Son may bring glory to the Father. You may ask me for anything in my name, and I will do it."* When I married my husband, he gave me his name, his checkbook, and later, a credit card. I use all of them...in the authority of his name. And I have a great time doing it! When I asked Jesus into my heart, through prayer, I became a daughter of the King—becoming royalty with all the privileges of inheritance. I was given the right to use my Father's name, asking anything in faith, believing my Father's promises. I use His name in praise, petition, proclamation, and power. He is my Father and He has given me the authority to pray His name. I am delighted by the privilege...using His name as well as His authority.

> *"To ask something in Christ's name means to ask by **His authority**. It means to ask on the basis of His character, according to the merit of His work, and by the power and right that He has personally given to us. It means that Jesus has lent His authority to us, giving us the right to pray according to His authority, which we have borrowed."*
>
> —Ray C. Stedman,
> *Talking with My Father*

Teach your children early that Jesus has invited them to use His blessed name when they pray.

Some say they just don't know how to pray. I would respond: "Do you know how to talk and listen? That works in prayer, also." A good place to begin to learn to pray would be in the Psalms. These are both prayers and songs.

Eugene Peterson, who wrote the wonderful Bible paraphrase called *The Message*, has opened new meaning for Bible readers in this major work. I have been using it since it came off the press in 1995. In the introduction of his Book of Psalms, Peterson says: "Most Christians for most of the Christian centuries have learned to pray by praying the Psalms." Peterson explains further that as a pastor, he was charged with the responsibility of teaching people to pray, and he found it difficult. He believes the impulse to pray is from deep within us—at the center of our created being. He says: "Faced with the prospect of conversation with a holy God who speaks worlds into being, it is not surprising that we have trouble. We feel awkward and out of place. 'I'm not good enough for this. I'll wait until I clean up my act and prove that I am a decent person.'" Peterson says his response to this is to put the Psalms in a person's hand and say:

"'Go home and pray these. You've got wrong ideas about prayer; the praying you find in the Psalms will dispel the wrong ideas about prayer and introduce you to the real thing.'... The Psalms in Hebrew are earthy and rough. They are not genteel. They are not the prayers of nice people, couched in cultured language.... I wanted to provide men and women access to the immense range and the terrific energies of prayer in the kind of language that is most immediate to them, which also happens to be the language in which these psalms prayers were first expressed and written by David and his successors."

He reminds his readers that Jesus Christ also prayed the Psalms. Reading Peterson's paraphrasing of the Psalms would be a good family exercise in teaching children to pray.

Many times, I've heard Dr. Billy Graham recommend the reading of one psalm per day to help us know God—and two proverbs a day to help us get along with each other. This is also a great legacy idea to leave your children and grandchildren.

Family Prayer Unites

I know of nothing that brings families closer together than prayer. When our prayers ascend to the Father, His power descends. Prayer is an expression of faith. True prayer is confidence, trust, and faith in God. Jesus invites us to pray. Remember: Jesus went alone to pray to His Father very often. Jesus knew from whence came the source of His power. It was from God, His Father. In John 5:19, Jesus said this about Himself: "*Truly, truly, I say to you, the Son can do nothing of Himself, unless it is something He sees the Father doing; for whatever the Father does, these things the Son also does in like manner*" (NASB). What a strong communication between the Father and the Son. This is a great example for us, as His children, to follow.

Prayer is a conversation between Father and child. Parenting is also like that! What the child sees the parent doing, they will also do. Create faith legacies...engraving upon your children an eternal inheritance. Matthew 18:19–20 (*The Message*) says: "*When two of you get together on anything at all on earth and make a prayer of it, my Father in heaven goes into action. And when two or three of you are together because of me, you can be sure that I'll be there.*"

To whom do we pray? Exodus 3:14–15 (AMP) tells us: "*And God said to Moses, I AM WHO I AM and WHAT I AM, and I WILL BE WHAT I WILL BE; and He said, You shall say this to the Israelites: I AM has sent me to you! God said also to Moses,*" (you have to love that He had a second thought when He added...) "*This shall you say to the Israelites: the Lord, the God of your fathers, of Abraham, of Isaac, and of Jacob, has sent me to you! This is My name forever, and by this name I am to be remembered to all generations.*"

Dear reader...when we pray, we are entering the very presence of WHO I AM, WHAT I AM, and WHAT I WILL BE. Get on your knees and cry *holy holy holy!* What a privilege!

The Creator of the universe invites you to speak with Him one-on-one. In Matthew's Gospel, chapter 18:19–20 (AMP), we are told; *"Again I tell you, if two of you on earth agree* (harmonize together, make a symphony together) *about whatever* [anything and everything] *they may ask, it will come to pass and be done for them by My Father in heaven. For wherever two or three are gathered* (drawn together as My followers) *in* (into) *My name, there I AM in the midst of them.*

Why Don't We Pray?

Prayer is the most intimate experience in one's life. When you are praying, you are in His presence. When couples pray, it is not just the two of you. You have entered the throne room of the King of kings, who is waiting for you, and that makes three! When we pray as families, remember—where two or three are gathered, He is in the middle.

Think of it like parents calling children to "huddle time" at the breakfast table. The family gathers in a huddle, with God in middle—He is waiting to hear your voice and eager to *coach* your family in Godly living. Gathered in this huddle around the kitchen table, reading God's Word, bowing before the "coach," to receive the day's "game plan."

Will, my daughter's husband and my son-in-love, stands at their breakfast nook and reads portions of the teen version of *My Utmost for His Highest* to his three daughters; then he gathers the girls and their mother to himself, and prays over and for them. This is indeed a sweet offering to God and a sweet legacy for his daughters that they will long remember.

Pray With and For Your Children

Our grandtwins had spent the night in our home. Early the next morning, Milligan found me upstairs in my "quiet place." I had my Bible and *Missions Mosaic* magazine open on my lap. Pointing to my open *Missions Mosaic* magazine, she asked:

"What is that, Nana?"

"That's my prayer book."

"Is my name in there?"

"This is the book Nana uses to pray for missionaries, just like we do at Nana Camp."

"Oh," she said, as she looked to see if her name was on the page.

I said: "Milligan, this is where I keep your name…right here in my prayer journal."

I opened my journal, showing her the page where her name was written.

"Oh, that's good, Nana! That's really good," she said with great authority.

My prayer is that she will grow to know that I pray for her daily...in His authority and His name. A *legacy of prayer* between a grandmother and granddaughter is an eternal issue. I believe that, as a grandmother, this is one of my jobs!

My brothers, sisters, and I have been given a huge prayer legacy. It is our richest inheritance from our parents and grandparents. Not only did my parents gather us at the table each morning for Bible reading and prayer, but through the years they have prayed together every morning for each child, each grandchild, and each great-grandchild...by name. To know you are being named in prayer before the throne is a priceless spiritual heritage. I tell my 99-year-old daddy that he can't quit yet! Not all his great-grandchildren know Jesus. I think prayer is the greatest legacy parents and grandparents can give to their children, and this will impact generations to come. Prayer is a spiritual legacy.

Scripture Praying

Let me suggest that you pray Scripture over your children. It might sound like this. Read out loud Proverbs 2:2 (NIV): *"turning your ear to wisdom and applying your heart to understanding."* Then, a prayer: "Father, Please allow the ears of _____ to be open to Your instruction through Your Word. Keep her ears from hearing the call to sin; teach her to listen to Your still, small voice. Draw her heart to Your understanding and wisdom. I pray in the strong name of Jesus, Amen."

Write these kinds of prayers to your child. Place them on their pillow, in their backpack, tape them to the bathroom mirror, and even attach them to their morning juice or milk glass. Start this habit early in the life of your child and they will come to cherish and rely on your prayers in their behalf. It will likely impact how they parent in years to come.

Elisabeth Elliot, one of my favorite writers, has an online daily devotion from one of her books. This story is from her book, *Keep a Quiet Heart,* and was received from her daily online devotional:

> *A reader asks, "At what age were the children when your parents started family prayers? How long a passage was read?" I think they must have begun as soon as the first child was born. I am Number Two, and I can't remember a time when we did not have family prayers. All of us were included, the smaller ones sitting on laps. My father read from Hurlbut's* Story of the Bible *(wearing out three hardback copies!), just a page or so each morning. In the evening after dinner, he read the evening portion of* Daily Light, *which is pure Scripture (King James Version). The hymn came first...then reading ...then (in the mornings, because we were not around the table then) we knelt to pray, my father leading, all joining in the Lord's Prayer to close.*

For several years now, I have been asking God to show me a Scripture verse that I could pray over my family for the coming year. I have yet to tell them what verse or even that I am praying a verse over them. I have recorded it in my prayer journal. In 2003, I prayed Matthew 18:10 (NASB) over the grandchildren. It says:

> *"See that you do not despise one of these little ones, for I say to you that their angels in heaven continually see the face of My Father who is in heaven."*

What a powerful verse to pray for your grandchildren. I prayed this verse by naming each child and thanking God for *their* angels—who never take their eyes off God's face. This verse was empowering for me to trust them to God's care.

My prayer verse for my children for 2004 was a powerful verse of God's faithfulness and what I claimed for my children, from Joshua 21:45:

> *"Not a word failed of any good thing which the LORD had spoken to the house of Israel. All came to pass."*

Prayer Matters…in Family

In Robert Wolgemuth's book *The Most Important Place on Earth,* he tells of a prayer ritual in their family. "On Sunday mornings, we drive northeast on Interstate 4 toward church. When we get to the Anderson exit, we pray. We ask God's blessing on the worship service, on the ministers, and on our Sunday school classes. We ask our heavenly Father to prepare our hearts to meet Him."

What a great legacy idea! This centers the hearts and minds of those in the car on the coming Bible study and worship time. Remember, parents, it's never too late to begin making family traditions.

Often, my husband, Bob, will drive me to speaking events. Right before we pull the car out of the driveway, he reaches for my hand and prays for God's traveling mercy on us, that he will be a good driver, and that God will bless what is to happen in the event. In my growing-up home, my father always prayed before we started any trip. Have prayer…will travel. He always prayed for traveling mercies.

Recently, a lady picked me up at the airport for a speaking engagement. We got in the car and right before we took off (literally), she prayed this prayer: "Lord, put an angel on every wheel! We're outta here! Amen." And off we went. I laughed out loud and I suspect God smiled too at this very honest prayer…and did we ever need it! Choose a time and a destination often traveled by your family and begin this prayer idea. You'll be amazed at how God will bless your travel time.

Some time ago, Bob and I were sitting with our friends, Bob and Peggy Story, at Wednesday night church. Bob told me this story about their daughter. I asked them to allow me to share it with you.

As is our daily practice, Peg and I share a morning devotion and prayer. We always lift our family, children, grandchildren, and in-laws to God for their day and their lives. One of our grandsons, Ben, is a fourth grader, living in Atlanta, GA. He had shared with his mom that there were a couple of boys in his class and on the soccer team that were 'bullies.' Ben would sometimes really dislike going to class and would feign some form of sickness. Our daughter, Sande, shared this situation with her mom and me and asked for suggestions and prayer. We offered encouragement to Ben and said we would pray for him and his situation.

Each Thursday, I meet with a group of men early before work. We do Bible study and share prayer needs. On the next meeting, I shared with my group the need for prayer for God's help for Ben and those that bullied him and others. That very morning, Sande called her mom and told her that a strange thing happened that morning. As she was taking the youngest boys to school, a lady ran up to the side of Sande's vehicle. Sande recognized her as a friend who was in a Bible study a few years back. She said 'Sande, I am starting a new Bible study at my home this afternoon. Would you like to come?' Sande accepted and attended that afternoon.

After the study, the leader asked for prayer requests and two ladies said that they needed prayer because they knew that their sons, who were in the fourth grade, were being bullies to some other boys and they wanted to correct the situation and have their sons be better students and young men. Of course, Sande sat there with her mouth open and could hardly contain herself until it was her time to share. She shared that her son was one of the children being bullied and that she had been praying for God's intervention and a way to correct the problem. Both moms and Sande talked at length after the group meeting and prayed together. They worked out plans to have Ben be part of their family outing to Stone Mountain the following Monday.

Sande immediately recognized that God had answered her prayers. The other two moms saw God at work and, of course, Peg and I were overjoyed at God's response and work.

After telling me this story, Bob said to me: "Does prayer work? Yes, most certainly. Does it always work as we want? Not necessarily. Does it work according to God's plan and divine will? If we ask in faith, trusting God—yes!"

Answered prayer becomes a family legacy! Answered prayer encourages prayerful living! Parents' and grandparents' prayer allows God to be actively at work in our families. Celebrate together as you see God working in your homes, and you will be teaching your children spiritual truth that later becomes their heritage.

It seems to me that prayer should be an everyday event, exercising spiritual traditions with your children. It needs to be a central focus in family…as important as *breathing*.

Why Don't We Pray?

Thanksgiving 2003, my twin brother David and his precious wife Pat were guests in our home. Our son David and his family joined us for the traditional Thanksgiving dinner. The past year was difficult because our families had faced very serious struggles and decisions, often putting us on our knees. A Thanksgiving tradition in our home is to always have a time of worship after the meal. I decorated the table with candles, for beauty and worship. Bob led us in expressions of gratitude, and as we recounted the past year in our lives, each person lit a candle for a specific answered prayer. It was such a sweet time of tearful celebration for God's faithfulness in all situations. Prayer enriches and binds families.

When our daughter Melody told us the grand news that we were to become grandparents, in great delight, I began knitting a baby blanket. All three of our granddaughters have received such a baby blanket, and yes, their dolls also received a mini-blanket.

Naturally, I would do the same for our son. On faith, asking God for a family for our son and his wife, I began knitting another baby blanket. You understand—they had not asked me to do so! I just love knitting! As I would knit, I would pray Scripture over each repeated pattern. By this time, we had three granddaughters. I was bold enough to ask God for a grandson...to carry on the *Burroughs* name. I journaled the Scriptures that I prayed over that blanket.

I was almost finished with the blanket when the phone call came that our son and his wife Colleen were expecting. *Yes!* Another call came two weeks later with more good news. Twins were on the way!

Leave legacies for your children and your grandchildren. Think of their future and what legacy you could make for them.

I started another blanket immediately and also covered it in prayer. Before the twins were born, I wrote each one a hand-written letter, delivered to the parents, to be opened on their fifteenth birthday, encouraging them with the Scriptures I had been praying over their lives. God gave us Milligan, a girl, and Walker, a boy!

Leave legacies for your children and your grandchildren. Think of their future and what legacy you could make for them. It might be a great time to learn to knit— I am speaking to you, be you aunt, friend, mom, godparent, or grandparent—so you can pass along the comfort of a blanket with a prayer heritage. Yes, prayer covers smocking, heirloom sewing, needlepoint, cross stitch, music, and all other arts—blessings, engraved by creative hands, touching another generation.

Family Connections, Prayer Suggestions

Here are some suggestions that might connect your family with prayer:

1. Have an email list of family members and relatives, and on a monthly or "by need" basis, share prayer requests and answers, to keep families connected by prayer.

2. Ask a family with the same makeup as yours to be prayer partners for a year. Each person in your family prays for the corresponding person in the other family. Share requests, so you know how to pray, and share how God answers your prayers—this will teach the children to trust God. This activity will become a treasure in the spiritual stories of your family.

3. Begin a family tradition by singing a blessing for meal times. You might use these words to the tune of the "Doxology"…or make up your own words as a family:

Be present at our table, Lord
Be here and everywhere adored
Thy children bless and grant that we
May eat and drink to honor Thee. Amen.

4. Bedtime prayers—teach your children to choose for whom they will pray, such as a family member, a missionary family, a relative, or a friend. Then allow that child to choose the next family member to pray. It sounds like this: "...(prayer)...Amen. I choose Mommy." Part of this ritual becomes *kisses all around.* The Emory Gaskins family, missionaries in Hong Kong, has used this method through the years with their children. It is indeed a lovely legacy.

5. Choose a familiar song and sing together to close prayer time with children. There are many recordings of prayer songs available in your local Christian bookstore. This is a good place to begin.

Recently I received an email from my Canadian Uncle Jack. He had written a letter for my father on his 98th birthday, December 2004. It read:

> *Congratulations on a wonderful 98 years! And our very best wishes for a very happy birthday! What an example you have set for us all! You are indeed, a "Statesman for the Lord." May He continue to bless you and may the next year be even more blessed for you and yours.*
>
> *When we received Esther's letter, asking for birthday submissions, we were pleased to be included. I immediately went to a photograph album that my dad received as a Christmas present from Uncle Bill in 1923. As I looked through the album, a*

flood of memories came to me. I was born in 1933 and I spent many happy summers on the farm. Even as a child, I was always mindful of the rich Christian heritage in the Milligan family. I remember the Sunday afternoons when the family knelt beside chairs at the kitchen in prayer. This was my first experience with private/group prayer. I was young during that time, less than ten years of age. But the experience was strong and impressive on my young heart. And not too many years later, I accepted Christ and have walked with Him ever since.

Reading my Uncle Jack's letter brought an engraved memory back to my heart. During the many holidays spent on the farm, the ritual was always the same. For mealtime, we gathered around the table and we prayed. No wonder my parents prayed for us around our table. My father was doing exactly what he saw his father doing! They were passing the legacy of family prayer from one generation to another.

Be Careful What You Pray

- Moses' prayers became God's reason to change His mind (Exodus 32:14).
- Abraham's prayer became the chosen people (Genesis 21:2).
- Jacob's prayer became a ruler of Egypt (Genesis 41:38).

- Naomi's prayer became the redeemer-kinsman (the Book of Ruth).
- Esther's prayer became the salvation of the Jews (the Book of Esther).
- Hannah's prayer became a prophet (1 Samuel 1:11).
- Hezekiah's prayer became a 15-year life guarantee (2 Kings 20:5–6).
- Daniel's prayer became a prisoner-prince (Daniel 6:10).
- David's prayer became a clean heart (Psalm 51).
- Zechariah's prayer became a man sent from God (Luke 1:13).
- Mary's prayer became the King of kings (Luke 2)!
- Paul's prayer became a "light to the Gentiles" (Ephesians 3:1–6).

How will God answer in the generations to come, because of your prayers?

Why Don't We Pray?

In December 2004, my father celebrated his 98th birthday. This past January, his only sister had her 101st birthday! Now that's a living legacy. Eunice, my father's wife, planned a big party for him at their church, First Baptist Church, Pell City, AL. They are loved by this church family. We sent word, inviting all of our family. Thirty-five family members came from Canada, Montana, Texas, South Carolina, and Alabama.

In tandem with this celebration, my father had been writing a book of prayers. I would love to give you the privilege of being in a gathering where Rev. D.G. Milligan voiced a prayer. With such proper use of the "King's English," as we said in Canada, an enormous knowledge of Scripture, and a very tender heart for God, he takes you to the throne room of grace, and you hear him speak intimately with God, his Father, as if they were dear and close friends—which they are!

I bless You, God, for my dad's faithfulness. A life, bookmarked by prayer...morning and evening. What a legacy!

One morning, after such a prayer in his Sunday school class, he was encouraged by a friend to write out his prayers and put them in a book. Now that is a radical thought for a man of God who is 98 years old and had never written out a prayer in his life! We encouraged him to consider it. He said he would pray about it. God led him through the Scripture to write one hundred prayers.

The journey began. My father has sight in only one eye. With the assistance of a magnifying glass, he wrote line after line, each prayer written first in his beautiful long-hand, and then typed lovingly by his wife Eunice. The finished book, *Prayers of the Heart*, was published in late

November of 2004. The prayers are Scripture and adoration of God's sovereignty. I love his oft-used closing words: "In the lovely name of Jesus."

I was visiting in the Texas home of my parents during the 1988 Winter Olympics, which took place in Calgary, Alberta, Canada. We enjoyed the women's ice skating competition, and of course we were cheering for the U.S. skater, Debbie Thomas. She had done well all year but was not able to win the gold medal. When she fell during her routine, my father got up and went back to the bedroom to prepare for bed. My mom and I hung on a little longer and then we too quit for the night. Making my way to the other bedroom in their home, passing their room, I saw my father, in his pajamas, kneeling beside his bed in prayer. My heart cried within me: *I bless You, God, for my dad's faithfulness*. A life, bookmarked by prayer…morning and evening. What a legacy!

Why don't we pray?

- it's work
  - it's hard work
    - it's life work

- it takes faith…and that's an eternal issue!
  - it takes hope…and that's a trust issue!
    - it takes love…and that's a grace issue!

- think of prayer as breathing
  - think of prayer as listening
    - think of prayer as asking...
      ...any thing
      ...at any time
      ...in any place
      ...in any way
      ...in the name of the Name that is above every name!

Legacies
⸺ OF PRAYER

- Bless your children today with prayer.

- Pray Scripture over your child sleeping in the crib.

- Begin bedtime prayers when children are infants.

- Purchase *The Message* by Eugene Peterson and begin praying the psalms together.

- Have your children write out their prayers.

- Keep Christmas cards; choose one each day and pray for that family.

- Use email prayer chains to keep family in touch.

- Adopt a prayer family, and pray for each other daily.

- Make a "Prayer Huddle" a family event.

- Pray over children before they leave for school.

Resources

1. *Prayer: Finding the Heart's True Home*
   by Richard Foster, published by Harper San Francisco

2. *Talking with My Father: Jesus Teaches on Prayer*
   by Ray C. Stedman, published by Discovery House
   Publishers

3. *The Message: The Bible in Contemporary Language*
   by Eugene Peterson, published by NavPress

4. *Keep a Quiet Heart* by Elisabeth Elliot,
   published by Vine Books

5. *Treasures of a Grandmother's Heart: Finding Pearls of
   Wisdom in Everyday Moments* by Esther Burroughs,
   published by New Hope Publishers

6. *The Most Important Place on Earth: What a Christian
   Home Looks Like and How to Build One*
   by Robert Wolgemuth, published by Nelson Books

7. *Prayers of the Heart* by Rev. D.G. Milligan (available
   from dgmilligan@visionsix.com)

chapter seven

Legacies of Holy Habits and Family Rituals

Bob and I spent Christmas 2001 with our son's family in Birmingham, Alabama. What fun we had with their then-three-year-old twins! David's wife, Colleen, had placed a wood-carved nativity on the fireplace hearth for the twins to enjoy. Milligan took the baby Jesus from the stable and, cradling it in her hands, walked over to show me the Christ Child. "Nana, you want hold baby Jesus?" Not waiting for my answer, she placed the carved figure in my hands. As quickly as she had placed it there, she took it back and returned it to the stable. She then said, "Nana, you want hold Mary, baby Jesus?" She placed the Mary figure in my hands. I knew "Joseph, baby Jesus" was not far behind!

That was a sweet holy moment for this Nana. I pondered in my heart her words—and my thoughts: *Emmanuel, God with us*. Indeed! By the Holy Spirit, Mary's body housed the Son of God, and her heart's love embraced the Son of God, her Savior. What a miracle—for Mary, and for you and me! Just as the Holy Spirit placed Jesus inside Mary, He also invites you and me to place Jesus Christ inside our lives as our Savior and Lord. Like Mary, we have the privilege of housing the Son of God in our lives, and therefore, in our homes. May we respond in obedience, as Mary: *"Behold the maidservant of the Lord! Let it be to me according to your word"* (Luke 1:38, NKJV).

It is Christ in us that makes our homes Christ-centered. With the person of the Holy Spirit indwelling, teaching, encouraging and correcting us, we can establish Christ-centered homes. My granddaughter was correct: "You want hold Esther, baby Jesus?" Put your name in place of my name!

Parents Teaching Spiritual Formation

Consider this truth: the home is God's first established institution! It was not the church. The church assists in this task.

On our 37th wedding anniversary, Bob and I attended a Marriage Encounter Weekend, sponsored by a Catholic

Church. Bob's desire was to go to Jamaica! But instead he chose to spend this weekend in Atlanta with me! Marriage Encounter is a well-established international marriage ministry, with the sole purpose of strengthening marriages. The weekend program of forty-four hours was presented by Christian laypersons whom I found so engaging...people just like you and me, who have the same struggles and are on the same journey. One of the overwhelming truths of the weekend that refreshed my thinking was this: Your home is a "little church" and you are the "light of Christ" in your neighborhood.

This is a wonderful spiritual concept. I had not heard it said just this way before. Why had I not thought of this? Scripture teaches this truth. Do you recall that the first thing Noah did, as he exited the Ark, was to build an altar for family worship? Noah was the priest in his home. The Old Testament priests went before God, offering sacrifice on behalf of the people of God.

In his book mentioned earlier, Robert Wolgemuth says:

> *Before God assigned priests to official duty, heads of households were the priest in their homes. Then, through the tribe of Levi and the family of Aaron, God authorized official priests to bring the nation of Israel before the throne of God. Then Jesus Christ stepped in as our Great High Priest and at the close of His ministry, passed the responsibility of the priesthood back to us in what we refer to as "The Great Commission."*

God's word clearly teaches parental responsibility for the spiritual formation of children in the family. Remember the words of Peter in Peter 2:9: *"But you are a chosen race, a royal priesthood, a holy nation, a people for God's own possession, that you may proclaim the excellencies of Him who has called you out of darkness into His marvelous light"* (NASB).

There it is…our job description as parents and grandparents! Claiming our priesthood, our holiness, in Christ, to be a light in our home and neighborhood because *"He called us out of darkness into his marvelous light."* This is a God assignment! You who know me also know that I am very passionate about passing on the baton of faith to the generations to come. It is a God assignment.

Robert Wolgemuth also says: "We are the proprietors of the most important place on earth. We are the specialists. No one can do this better than we can. No one is more qualified." He also suggests that perhaps a sign should be placed in all our front yards with these words:

> *A Christian Home*
> *Dad and Mom—Priests*
> *Worship Services Daily*

Begin early establishing patterns, rituals, and traditions that will become meaningful life lessons in the lives of your children.

In my growing up home, Sunday was called the Lord's Day or Sabbath. Sabbath day rituals were always the same…consistent…never-changing. In "big church," our family sat in the first pew, piano side. Only PKs (preacher kids) could understand *the look* in the eyes of their daddy, from the pulpit and yes, even while he was preaching! If we misbehaved in big church, Mother would pinch our ears, and that meant we received a spanking after church. I was almost a grown woman before I realized that a spanking was not on the order of worship in our church!

Our home was made orderly by my parents. We had "Sunday" clothes and shoes and we had "school" clothes and shoes. Our Sabbath rituals included the concept that everything for Sunday had to be ready on Saturday night. For instance:

- Clothes were pressed and placed on hangers.
- Shoes were shined and socks were ready to wear.
- Bible and offering envelopes were laid out.
- Sunday School lessons were prepared.
- The Sunday dinner was prepared on Saturday night.
- The table was set with tablecloth and our best dishes. It was a family affair.

Sunday was also a day for quiet in our home, so our Preacher Daddy could take a nap. In all my childhood years, Sabbath rituals/traditions never changed. Rules were kept and they were simple:

- No playing! We did have Sunday toys—which were quiet games, such as puzzles.
- We could, of course, read the Bible, and books such as *The Sugar Creek Gang,* or *The Hardy Boys* were acceptable.

There were also weekday rules in my home. Here are just a few:

- Children were to be seen and not heard.
- Manners were "in."
- Everyone does chores.
- Respect your elders.
- Never say "Shut up."
- Remember the Sabbath day to keep it holy.
- Always tell the truth.
- Do your best and then some.
- Finish what you begin.
- Everyone took some type of music lessons.
- Study hard for good grades.
- And most important of all:
  always remember: You are a Milligan!

I always felt like that last rule came straight from the mouth of my grandmother, and we were taught to live in such a way as to bring honor to the family name. That may be old-fashioned, but I choose to feel that a high standard was set for us by our parents and grandparents, teaching us that the Heavenly Father also called us to show His resemblance in our family by honoring and obeying Him.

In Biblical times, parents blessed their children with a physical touch...a spoken touch...and words of affirmation. In Jewish tradition, the father assumed primary responsibility for training the child. The Jewish law states: *"It is the duty of every father to train his children in the practice of all the precepts."* My parents parented us—based their love and care for us from Proverbs 22:6: *"Train up a child in the way he should go, and when he is old he will not depart from it."*

To a strict Jew, that meant the way of his father and his father's father before him. Every Jewish child learned Deuteronomy 4:6-9. Parents taught their children God's law as instructed in Deuteronomy 6:1-9.

Holy Habits Create Sacred Space in Family

In today's fast-paced world, families need a *withdrawing room*—a place to ponder and refresh. Please allow me to suggest some ideas that might be of help to today's busy parents:

- Make some part of your week a preparation time for worship on Sunday, Friday or Saturday—depending when your church family meets for worship.
- Make this a fun time for your family.
- Gather all the Bibles and Sunday School material.
- Match shoes with socks…shoes shined and ready to wear.
- Get Sunday clothes ready and on hangers in each child's room.
- Have music playing that the whole family enjoys during this time.
- Music lifts the heart toward God and always refreshes the inner spirit.

When the tasks are done and everything is ready for Sabbath, take a moment and pray together (which, of course, is part of worship) for your church. This kind of preparation will deliver a more peaceful Sunday morning and worship day. It could become a family ritual. Rituals that begin early in a child's life make it easier to keep as children get older. Rituals will always need updating as related to the age of your children and their physical and spiritual needs.

The rhythm of Sunday is very different from that of the weekdays. God Himself designed Sabbath for our spiritual nurture and a time to be recreated in His presence. How desperately our busy culture needs a day of rest, balanced with work days. Being refreshed by worship is like taking a deep breath of refreshing spring air—it refocuses our lives.

> *"Thus the heavens and the earth were finished, and all the host of them. And on the seventh day God ended His work which He had done: and He rested on the seventh day from all His work which He had done."* —Genesis 2:1-2 (NKJV)

> *"And God blessed* [spoke good of] *the seventh day, set it apart as His own, and hallowed it, because on it God rested from all His work which He had created and done."* —Genesis 2:3 (AMP)

Exodus 20 gives God's clear command about Sabbath. In verses 8-9, it says:

> "[Earnestly] *remember the Sabbath day, to keep it holy* [withdrawn from common employment and dedicated to God]. *Six days you shall labor and do*

*all your work, but the seventh day is a Sabbath to
the Lord your God; in it you shall not do any work,
you, or your son, your daughter, your manservant,
your maidservant, your domestic animals, or the
sojourners within your gates." (AMP)*

Verse 11:

*"That is why the Lord blessed the Sabbath day and
hallowed it* [set it apart for His purposes]." (AMP)

I am convinced that if families made an effort to treat the
Lord's Sabbath day as a set-apart day, we would find a rest
that would fuel us through the week. Yes, I know in our
culture that Sunday is a very busy day…especially at church.
I am suggesting you can choose to worship in your church
and then, make clear family choices on how your family will
spend the afternoon and evening hours of Sabbath.

Author Karen Mains, in her book *The Heart of a Sabbath
Keeper*, says these words:

*The average churchgoing Western Christian has
lost something very important—a concept of the
holiness of time. One reason for this is that we
are not making the time of Sunday with Sabbath understanding. Sabbath is not a place we
go to perform rituals, but a time set aside to be
with God, ourselves, and others. All days are
holy, but some are more so; all moments can be*

sacred but not unless we set some aside to be intensely so.

Always be looking for ways to establish worship traditions/rituals in your home. Look for those holy moments in the life of your family Sunday through Saturday and celebrate them as *holy!*

Again, taking experiences from my growing-up home, every morning before school, our family gathered around the breakfast table and before eating, my father read from the Bible. At that time in my life, it felt like he was reading *all* of the Old Testament! After father read, we knelt by our chairs for prayer time. Each child was prayed for by name, as were all our missionary friends. When father said the final *Amen,* we then were allowed to eat our breakfast. In our home, this was known as *family altar.* For all the eighteen years I lived with my parents, this holy habit never varied. It was as much a part of my legacy as my name: Esther Ruth Milligan.

My mother's personal time of worship included Bible reading and prayer. She was indeed a woman of prayer. One day, in a visit with her before she passed away, she asked me this question:

"Esther, do you ever speak to minister's wives?"

"Yes, sometimes," was my reply.

"Well, I shared with a group of young women recently that every Sabbath morning, I would lay out your Father's clothes on the bed for him—his suit, tie, hanky, socks and shoes."

She told me she was somewhat surprised when they laughed at her comments, but she had not intended them to be humorous! Their laughter was wrapped in this response: *Let them dress themselves!*

"I remember you did that for Dad. Why did you do it?" I asked her. I thought that might be a rule in some Minister's Wife Handbook! She quietly replied with these piercing words:

"I did it so that your Father could have more time in prayer before God as he prepared to go to the pulpit and open the Word of God for the people of God."

I wonder what might happen in our homes today if family members made an effort to allow for *holy space* as each one gets ready for worship. I wonder!

After mother's death in 1996, I was given her prayer journals. She was amazing! She simply put her request on the left side of the page and when God answered, she dated the answer on the right side of the page! While reading these precious journals—written on dime-store binders, I laughed and cried. She had prayed me out of several relationships. She prayed over every opportunity God had provided Bob and me. How faithful she was before the Lord on behalf of her family. Indeed, she gave us a true spiritual heritage.

The Reason for Family Worship

Family Worship is looking for opportunities to see eternal significance in everyday matters.

Family Worship is seeing the sacred in the ordinary, and catching the moment.

Family Worship builds tradition and builds family togetherness.

Family Worship develops holy habits and spiritual disciplines which help families experience God.

Here are seven basic reasons for family worship:

1. The purposes of God
2. The place of God
3. The presence of God
4. The blessings of God
5. The faithfulness of God
6. The promises of God
7. The commands of God for the family

Let's look at each one:

1. The Purposes of God

As a small child, I was taught a little song with these words:

A Sunbeam, a Sunbeam
I'll be a sunbeam for Jesus
To please Him in every way
at home, at school, at play.

Our purpose is to please God—to find favor in His sight! Moses prayed this prayer in Exodus 33:13: *"Now therefore, I pray Thee, if I have found favor in Thy sight, let me know Thy ways, that I may know Thee, so that I may find favor in Thy sight,"* (NASB). This is a wonderful family prayer! *Let us know Your ways, O God, so we will know You!* Family worship allows for *God stops* in our homes—finding favor with God and helping us to know and trust God.

In the summer of 1998 we conducted our first Nana's summer camp—eight years ago, and we had a time of worship and fulfilling God's purpose in family. The camp theme was "I Am a Promise! I Am a Possibility!"

My favorite time was the birthday breakfast for our three grandgirls. Since Bob and I are seldom with them on the real birthdays, we decided to have an extra birthday for them—all at one time. Anna, our oldest grandgirl, helped Bop (Bob's grandfather name) fix his World Famous Bop's Breakfast.

After the meal and before we gave their gifts, each person was given a sheet of paper on which was drawn a gift box, wrapped in a bow with a tag that read: You are special. Anna had written the name of each person on the left hand side of the gift box. I instructed everyone at the table to give a word gift to each family member...by writing a descriptive word beside the name of each person. When finished, each person around the table read the word gift they had written for each family member. It was, indeed, a holy moment!

In Anna's creativity, she had written *Twin #1* and *Twin #2* at the bottom of the page, because we were all excited that our son, David, and his wife were expecting twins in September, 1998. Most of us wrote the word *thankful* on the twins' sheets as we had prayed for these babies and a healthy arrival. Caroline, the middle granddaughter, in her sensitivity, wrote the word *hopeful* by twin #1 and twin #2. I cried. Bop then prayed a blessing, naming quality traits of each person at the table, and a special blessing on the expected twins and their parents. A birthday breakfast becomes an altar of thanksgiving, and we found God's favor as we met with Him that morning.

USA Today reported some time ago that children spend an average of 38.5 hours a week watching TV and movies, and playing computer and video games. It also said that parents talk to children about 37 seconds a day, and to each other about 7 minutes a day. Consider these facts:

- The average kindergarten graduate has already spent nearly 6,000 hours watching television—more time than it takes to obtain a bachelor's degree!
- The average American child is bombarded with an estimated 20,000 30-second TV commercials each year.

How can we possibly teach them God's laws and God's ways in that kind of time frame? We can't! It is impossible. I am suggesting that we must counter the culture with quality family time. Family altar—on a regular basis—can and will help overcome the influence of our culture, but it must be the parents who make the choice to limit the use of TV and other distractions.

"I don't want to do family altar!" Perhaps your child has said these words. In our home, our children did not have a choice in the matter of family altar. It is one of those parent-control activities. You can proclaim it by virtue of being the parent, and it wields power in the fact that a tradition does not have to be explained—just done. We used the calendar year to help make preparation for family altar in our home. For example, we have always had a worship service following our Thanksgiving meal, Christmas dinner, individual birthdays, and more. Be creative. Get a resource book and fill yourself with ideas that will work for your family altar.

2. The Place of God

When King David wanted to build a house for God, he was reminded by the prophet Nathan: *"Go and tell David, my servant, 'Thus says the Lord: You shall not build Me a house to dwell in, for I have not dwelt in a house since the day that I brought up Israel from Egypt until this day: but I have gone from tent to tent, and from one tabernacle to another.'"* God has always tented (dwelt) with his people.

The place for family altar can be rather simple. It can be as simple as choosing the place where the family gathers frequently. The place can and should vary...but the habit must be consistent. Here are some suggestions and examples as to where to have family altar and what you might include:

• **The Bedroom**—with nighttime prayers and Bible and other stories. I know one family that allows each child to choose two books each evening and one of the two books must be a Bible story book.

• **The Kitchen Table**—seemingly, the practice of eating together as a family is about to be lost! Family experts tell us that today the only night the entire American family is usually together ...is Sunday night! A Sunday evening, then, can be a great time for family night and family worship.

When our son, David, was a college freshman, he and his friends had the privilege of leading his roommate to know Christ. Jim Bush became a frequent visitor in our Atlanta home. While I prepared dinner, Jim would sit on a stool at the counter, visiting with me while I peeled potatoes. His questions were endless. He had not grown up in a Christian home. He was so thirsty to know how to walk with God. I cherished these visits though I did not have all the answers. We adopted Jim to our hearts and welcomed him in our home as often as possible. The November of 1994, David brought Jim and Sandy (his new bride) and Nate Hansen home for Thanksgiving with us when we lived in West Palm Beach, FL. We were excited that we would have our kids home for the Thanksgiving holidays. We waited for them to be with us so we delayed the dedication of our home to the Lord for this occasion. Before the Thanksgiving meal, we gathered at the front door, and as we went to each room, scripture was read that related to the room. Then we prayed for the room to be used for God's glory. Bob had assigned me the dining room to dedicate. As we stood around the table, I said, "We are so happy to have you in our home to celebrate this holiday with us. Jim told me early this morning that he missed our Atlanta home and our visits at the kitchen counter." Jim interrupted me, saying: "The counter? I always called that an altar." Whew! Indeed a kitchen counter becomes an altar!

When our children were growing up, we had Burroughs Family Night every Friday. Each family member took turns choosing the activity one evening per month. I must admit, bowling was my least favorite family event! All of our family planned and helped prepare the meal for this special evening, including setting and clearing the table, or occasionally selecting a restaurant, with everyone sharing in the table conversation.

For a period of time, the family member who told the funniest story from their week received $1.00—placed on the refrigerator with a magnet. This little incentive helped ensure table conversation. Of course, a dollar in the '70s went further than it goes today! You might have to up the incentive! We found this an excellent time to discuss issues that affected our family, school, church and community. On those evenings, we planned worship after the evening's event. Most family events are opportunities for altar times, building family unity in Christ, and building family memories.

The kitchen table is considered the center of a home. It seems that this is where everything is dumped. Think about it!

- back packs after school
- sports bags and equipment
- groceries from the market
- library books
- heartaches
- relationship problems
- joys
- failures

How about turning that kitchen table into an altar? Oh, I know it doesn't look like an altar most of the time, but if it is where we find love, concern, kindness, prayer and a Bible verse, then a *dumped-on-table* becomes an *altar*.

Make meal time sacred. When everyone around the dinner table participates in conversation, prayer, blessing, or thanksgiving, then a table has become an altar, and memories become legacies.

• **The Family Room**—where the TV and entertainment center must be silenced. That reminds me of a time when our children were in grade school and our TV was broken. It was several weeks before the TV was returned to our family room. Upon its return, our son said these astounding words: "I wish the TV was still broken—because we talked to each other more often and played games together." That was amazing insight from a child who already watched limited TV and had no video games, but it was a profound truth. Without the noise and distraction of the TV, we talked to each other more. You will find many opportunities for altar times in the family room.

Depending on the ages of the children, have a movie night, choosing movies that teach family values. After viewing the video, have a family dialogue about the truths that were taught. Relate this to a recent family situation, if possible. Open the word of God as often as you can to teach your children reliance on God's promises and principles. Close the evening with prayer—always giving the children an opportunity to pray. Celebrate God's presence in your family.

Show family videos. Children love to see themselves as babies and young children. This is a great time to give a simple prayer of gratitude for God's favor on your family.

Any place in your home, indoor or outdoor, where all the family can meet is a good place for worship. The purpose is about meeting together as a family to worship and the place is about His place in our hearts.

3. The Presence of God

I recently saw a church marquee sign that read: "The ultimate sanctuary is not a place...but a person." Matthew 18:20 reminds of God's presence in us, therefore in our homes: *"For wherever two or three are gathered* [drawn together as My followers] *in* [into] *My name, there I AM in the midst of them"* (AMP). What a great promise from Jesus to your family. It is the same promise God made to the children of Israel in Exodus 3:14,15b, His chosen family:

> *"And God said to Moses, 'I AM WHO I AM and WHAT I AM, and I WILL BE WHAT I WILL BE;' and He said, 'You shall say this to the Israelites, I AM sent me to you. This is My name forever, and by this name I am to be remembered to all generations.'"*
> (AMP)

Praise God! This verse is for you and me in this generation. I believe God is counting on us to pass the baton of faith to generations yet to be born!

4. The Blessings of God

As you have previously read, Bob and I have always dedicated our homes to the Lord. Our home does not belong to us. It belongs to the Mortgage Company! We are to be stewards of the home and use it in such a way that it will be a blessing to the Father.

When we moved into our home in West Palm Beach, FL, where Bob was to begin his teaching at Palm Beach Atlantic University, we bought an older home that was near the Intercoastal Waterway. We pulled up the carpets and found wonderful hardwood floors. We then looked for someone to sand and finish them. We found the best in town! What a delight to discover, as we went in and out to check on the progress, the gospel was being heard. Jerry Knuckles, the gentleman sanding and finishing our floors, would sing praises to the Lord at the top of his lungs with the windows wide open...and the neighbors heard! At times, he would stop singing and begin praying. While I was unpacking boxes in the room that was to be my office, Jerry was putting the finishing touches on the dining room floor and...singing, of course. He stopped singing and began to pray. I stopped to listen.

He prayed, "Father, I consecrate this dining room floor to you. I've done my best and I've used my gifts, but now I consecrate these floors to You and pray that everybody that comes in Bob and Esther's home and sits around their table will feel the love of God." Then he got up and prayed over the living room, the bedroom and continued as he consecrated each room in the house.

"Father," I prayed, "You know we always dedicate our home to You but I've never had anyone consecrate our home before we moved in. Thank You." Finishing his job,

Jerry stopped praying and moved out of the kitchen and through the garage. I knew he was coming to the front door and I did not know whether to tell him I'd been a part of his worship service or not, but it was so obvious as the tears ran down my face. I said, "Oh. Jerry! Bob and I thank you for consecrating our home to the Lord!" Indeed, it was an altar of thanksgiving!

Your home does not need to be new! Even if you have lived in it for some time, plan a special time of worship with family and friends to dedicate your home to God, asking for His blessings, honor, and for your witness. A great time to do this, if you haven't done it, is the season of Thanksgiving!

To have a successful family altar, it must be put on the family calendar—along with other important dates. Once it is placed on this calendar, you are less likely to forget and it adds significance to the occasion.

Don't be discouraged! If you have never done this before and are just now thinking about beginning, you can do it. Call the family together and share with them that you want to be obedient to God in leading your family in scriptural truth. You may wish to say that you are sorry that as a family, we have not done this in our home before, but you...and the family...are choosing to begin today. Little children will accept it. Teens may not like it, but they will most likely eventually feel more safe and loved by your care to begin a family altar time.

Anytime is a good time to begin. Begin slow. Most families could not do family altar today as my parents did for the obvious reason that today's family schedules are more hectic and families seldom eat together around the table! If you carefully plan to do worship, say twice a month, you will probably do it twice a month. Family altar does not have to mean that all family members are present every time. A mother/son afternoon of shopping and a quiet dinner together...a father/daughter planned time with the intention of sharing meaningful life conversations and a promise of prayer about ideas discussed, or prayer at their bedside is certainly one of the ideas behind family altar. Make God's blessings to you a gift to your children and yes, the generations yet to come.

5. The Faithfulness of God

Isaiah 38:19 says: *"It is the living who give thanks to Thee, as I do today; a father tell his sons about Thy faithfulness."* Dads: That's your job! I recently became acquainted with the Jesse Tree celebration for the Advent Christmas season. It is a wonderful way to teach Scripture and the God story to your family. The basic idea is that the life of Jesus is traced from the very beginning of time and through all the prophecies—telling of His coming.

Isaiah 11:1 says: *"Then a shoot will spring forth from the stem of Jesse, and a branch from His roots and will bear fruit."* The Jesse Tree banner is a symbolic way of portraying the spiritual heritage of Jesus. It is to be used during the Advent season. In order to finish the tree on Christmas Day, the first scripture and study should be read on November 27, as the banner is hung in a place where it can be seen by family and friends. There is a symbol for each day's study.

Attach the symbol for the day to the Jesse Tree banner. Reserve the top of the tree for Christmas Day! This is a great way to do Family Advent! A Jesse Tree family celebration helps your children know the characteristics of God's faithfulness. You can do an Internet search of the words "Jesse Tree" and a multitude of information comes up, including how to do it, where to get materials, and much more!

6. The Promises of God to Families

Genesis 21:1-2 states: *"Now the LORD was gracious to Sarah as He had said, and the LORD did for Sarah what he **had promised**. Sarah became pregnant and bore a son to Abraham in his old age, at the **very time** God **had promised**,"* (NIV). And 1 Chronicles 11:3 tells us: *"When all the elders of Israel had come to King David, he made a compact with them at Hebron before the LORD, and they anointed David king over Israel, as the LORD had **promised** Samuel"* (NIV).

Regardless of what you see happening in our world today, and no matter what happens, remember this: God still keeps His promises. Keep telling the stories of God's faithfulness to your family. Tell your children your life stories often until they know them well enough to tell to their children...those stories will become their legacy! We know this because 1 Thessalonians 5:24 says: *"The one who calls you...is faithful and He will do it."*

7. The Commands of God for Families

Matthew 2:11 tells us of the three kings bowing in worship over the place where the child was. The light of the star guided their path to the baby king. *"On coming to the house, they saw the child with his mother Mary, and they bowed down and worshiped him. Then they opened their treasures and presented him with gifts..."*

Imagine such a scene—the Magi entering the stable, seeing the baby, bowing in worship. They carried gifts for the baby king and presented their gifts... *after* they had worshiped Him. Ponder worship...then gift-giving!

One Christmas, I planned our family Christmas dinner later in the day—to suit various travel schedules so little ones could do *Santa* in their own homes. My planning was with purpose. I announced we would open gifts after dinner. Gathered at the table, Bob opened the Bible and read the Luke 2 story. Then I asked the children to go throughout the house and gather the baby Jesus figures from every nativity scene, and to place one in front of each person at the table. After they had gathered them and placed each one, I said to those around our table: "Nana would like to ask you to do something we have never done before. As a little girl, my family prayed, kneeling beside our chairs. Today, I would like for us to get on our knees as we pray together." Quietly, the family knelt and Bob led us in prayer. After that, we opened our gifts. It was a most meaningful time together.

I certainly like what my pastor, Dr. Gary Fenton, says every Sunday in worship: "Now let's do the work of the church. You may sit, stand or kneel, whatever posture allows you to best do the work of the church." He then kneels to pray.

One of God's strongest commands to us is to pray. You choose a posture for your family worship time. Remember, family worship is a way of being the *little church* on your street. It is keeping the lamp of God on so this generation can impact the next generation...touching tomorrow ...today!

After we were married, my husband and I chose to celebrate the tradition of family altar differently from our families of origin. We firmly believe God's instruction in Deuteronomy 6: 1-9, from the NASB translation:

> *"Now this is the commandment, the statutes and the judgments which the LORD your God has commanded me to teach you, that you might do them in the land where you are going over to possess it, so that you and your son and your grandson might fear the LORD your God, to keep all His statutes and His commandments, which I command you, all the days of your life, and that your days may be prolonged.*
>
> *"Hear, O Israel! The LORD is our God, the LORD is one! And you shall love the LORD your God with all your heart and with all your might and with all your soul. And these words, which I am commanding you today, shall be on your heart; and you shall teach them diligently to your sons* [and daughters] *and shall talk of them when you sit in your house and when you walk by the way and when you lie down and when you rise up. And*

you shall bind them as a sign on your hand and they shall be as frontals on your forehead. And you shall write them on the doorposts of your house and on your gates."

Dear reader...that is *all* the time! We are to teach God's ways to our children in every part of our home!

Establishing Family Altar as Tradition

Traditions are simply beliefs and customs that are handed down from generation to generation. Traditions are passed from family to family, through the generations. Traditions connect us to our past—as well as our future. Traditions are just that...tradition! If you did not grow up with traditions, let me urge you to find out that it is never too late to begin.

How can we possibly do this in our fast-paced world? We are inundated by electronics and media that keep us far more connected than we would choose to be, giving us less time for family matters that should be.

My advice to all parents who are choosing modern technology over family and parenting is this:

**GO TO *TIME OUT*!
DON'T COME OUT UNTIL I TELL YOU!**

Just kidding! Actually, I am quite serious about this subject, though. Take time to think it through, while you are in time out. What is the most important thing in your family? Is it not time together?

The world has definitely changed, but children still come to us as gifts from God and need the sanctuary of home, family time, boundaries, nurture and certainly encouragement from parents. Parenting is the hardest job on earth. It is long, difficult and hard work. The beauty in all of this is that there are stages and seasons in parenting. It will not always be as hard as caring for newborns. It's even harder caring for teens! Parenting is a 24/7 job and I'm not kidding. As a grandmother, I am still vitally interested in my children, their spiritual journey, their parenting and for certain, their children. You never stop being a parent. The issue is finding a balance. I am suggesting to you, Dear Reader, that holy habits help us focus on what really matters … family!

What if we forget to live?

What if we don't leave legacies?

What if we miss God's instructions?

Are you taking time for family…first?

Laughter takes time
   Tears take time
      Discipline takes time
         Forgiveness takes time
            Projects take time
               Children take time

Vacations take time
Marriage takes time
Climbing trees takes time
Riding bikes takes time
Tea parties take time
Reading books takes time
Sport activity takes time
Picnics take time
Holy habits take time

Family takes time...everyone's time!

Will you take the time for family values?

Will this generation walk with God in family matters in such a way that God would say about your family what he said about King David's faithfulness: "*That my servant, David, may have a lamp always before Me in Jerusalem, the city where I chose for Myself to put My name that my servant* (your name _____) *may have a lamp always before Me,*" (1 Kings 11:36). What would God choose to save for another generation...because of your faithfulness?

The greatest gifts you can give your children are your presence with them and a rich, spiritual legacy.

Remember: This is your job!

Legacies

─ OF HOLY HABITS AND FAMILY RITUALS

- Have a family bedtime prayer ritual.
- Read contemporary biblical books as your family travels.
- Sing hymns/choruses together around the table or in the car.
- Design your own rituals to prepare for church each week.
- Use the monthly calendar to plan family worship times and events.
- Celebrate events in the church calendar, such as Advent and Lent, as family worship events.
- Celebrate spiritual birthdays as a family as well as physical birthdays.
- Bake a birthday cake for Jesus.
- Use a family night to tell the meanings/origin of your Christmas decorations.
- Prepare seasonal goodies for neighbors and friends and enclose a Bible promise.
- Memorize one scripture verse monthly.
- Have a family movie night and show a movie that. invites faith discussions.
- Have scrapbook viewing nights as a family, to teach the family story.

Resources

1. *The Most Important Place on Earth* by Robert Wolgemuth, published by Nelson Books

2. *Making Sunday Special* by Karen Mains, published by Word Publishing

chapter eight

Legacies of Grace

God accepts me…and that's grace.
I accept that God accepts me…and
  that's grace.
Now I accept me…and that's grace.
That frees me to accept you…and
  that's grace.
Free to live in grace with each
  other…and that's God's grace
  amazing.

          —Esther Burroughs

*H*er car was parked under a
tree in the farthest corner of
the church parking lot. Two small
children were playing in the back seat.

There's not much room in the back of a station wagon for children to play. Following the crowd, she made her way into the church that Wednesday evening. Finding the bathroom, she washed the children's faces and hands in the sink and dried them with rough paper towels. I'm glad my friend, Rose, was there to see her and invite her to supper in the church fellowship hall. I joined them for the meal. It was obvious the little ones were very hungry. We invited her back and she kept coming. After several visits, my husband, who was minister of music at the church, invited her to choir. She came, and often sat by me. I wondered where she lived and how she provided for her children. I learned that she lived much of her life on the street, in and out of jobs, and often using her body to buy food, a bed, and trying to maintain some kind of life.

Some weeks later, she came into choir rehearsal and I noticed one of the lenses in her glasses was missing. Her arms were bruised. I asked the obvious question: "What happened?" "I fell," she said. About the same time, the nursery ladies noticed bruises on the children. More than once, being put out of some man's house, she'd call for help to get her belongings out of the street, needing a place to spend the night. People from the church helped in every way possible until the day came that she had to be turned over to the authorities for the safety of the children. In need of some grace, she found herself without her children and living in the downtown women's homeless shelter. But through all of this turmoil in her life, she continued to come to dinner and choir.

I'll never forget that Sunday morning service. It is forever engraved in my mind. From my place in the choir loft, I watched as she paraded several children from the shelter down the center aisle. Congregational heads turned from every direction, following her path. Finding a pew at the front of the church, she settled them in and gathered them close to her side. As the service continued, my husband invited the congregation to stand and sing the familiar hymn, "Amazing Grace." As we began to sing, she gave each child a hymnal, and stood over them like a mother hen. We sang with all our hearts those familiar words:

Amazing grace, how sweet the sound
that saved a wretch like me.
I once was lost, but now I'm found,
was blind, but now I see.

After the worship service was over, she told me that when she stood the children to sing that hymn, a lady behind her whispered out loud: "Who does she think she is, bringing these kind of people into my church?" Looking into my heart, she said these words: "Anybody can *sing* "Amazing Grace." I'm looking for someone who *is* amazing grace!" I hope to never forget her words. A homeless mother brings homeless children to church. A church member says she doesn't belong.

There you have it! I'm guilty! Early in my ministry, I spent too many years working hard in the church trying to get God's approval (favor), not realizing God already approved….and that it was not about my rules. It was all about His *grace*.

I did not grow up in a church family that taught grace. It was all about the law. And it showed because there was very little joy in life. I still struggle between law and grace. I am in good company! I'm like Paul, *"For what I'm doing, I do not understand; for I am not practicing what I would like to do, but I am doing the very thing I hate…or I know that nothing good dwells in me, that is my flesh; for the willing is present in me, but the doing of the good is not"* (Romans 7:15-16, 18). In my own words:

> *I do what I don't want to do. I say what I don't want to say…and I know when I don't feel grace!*

I'd sure like to do some of my early years over, living in the delight of His amazing grace. I'm desperate to live as though dressed in grace, transformed in His likeness. I've spent too many years as a Pharisee, with stones in my pockets…ready for instant use.

I thank God that He kept putting grace people in my path, to show me the path of grace. Grace has already been given as gift, and I've been touched by grace over and over. I want to touch with grace, over and over. Don't get me wrong! I do have some grace, with some people, some of the time, in some circumstances. I'm thinking I should quit singing "Amazing Grace" until I get the *living* of amazing grace right! I don't know about you, but I find the home the hardest place to live transformed by *grace*.

"But God—so rich is He in His mercy! Because of and in order to satisfy the great and wonderful and intense love with which He loved us, even when we were dead in sin...He made us alive with Christ; He gave us the very life of Christ...it is by grace [His favor and mercy which you did not deserve] *that you are saved.*

"He did this that He might clearly demonstrate through the ages to come the immeasurable [limitless, surpassing] *riches of His free grace* [His unmerited favour] *in* [His] *kindness and goodness of heart toward us in Christ."*

"For it is free grace...not because of works [not the fulfilment of the Law's demands] *lest any man should boast...for we are God's* [own] *handiwork."*
—Ephesians 2:4, 5, 7–10 (AMP)

Grace is free...because of the cross! Whew!

God's grace has always been grace. He placed His grace in you and me by His Son, and desires that He has the freedom to live by grace in us, through the Holy Spirit. Dear reader, try, along with me, to cling daily to the surpassing riches of God's grace. Touched by grace!

Blessed by grace!

Amazed by grace!

Chosen by grace!

Forever, God has been the storyteller of redeeming grace. God's story is filled with chosen people through whom He continues to tell the grace story. His grace is unmerited favor upon His chosen. He is the God of the second chance and because of His grace upon a cross, we know His favor.

> *"The Lord did not set His love* [grace] *upon you and choose you because you were more in number than any other people, for you were the fewest of all people. But because the Lord loves you and because He would keep the oath which He had sworn to your fathers* [grace], *the Lord has brought you out with a mighty hand and redeemed you* [amazing grace] *out of the house of bondage, from the hand of Pharaoh, King of Egypt. Know, recognize, and understand therefore that the Lord Your God, He is God, the faithful God, who keeps covenant* [grace] *and steadfast love* [grace] *and mercy with those who love Him and keep His commandments, to a thousand generations."*
>
> —Deuteronomy 7:7–9
> The bracketed [grace] is my addition.

Grace is…love! Love is… grace! Father, teach me to love in Your grace and grace in Your love. Meet some of His favorite grace followers:

• God's amazing grace for Abraham was the promise of a son, along with a ram caught in a thicket by its horns….a blessing from God! *"Behold, God will provide for Himself the lamb,*" (Genesis 22:14). Abraham named the place Yahweh Jir'eh, the Lord will provide. Amazing grace!

• God's amazing grace for Moses was a basket and a cloud. "*Then the cloud* [called the Shekinah, it was God's visible presence] *covered the Tent of Meeting, and the glory of the Lord filled the Tabernacle! For throughout all their journeys the cloud of the Lord was upon the Tabernacle by day, and fire was in it by night, in the sight of all the house of Israel,*" (Exodus 40:34, 36). Amazing grace!

• God's amazing grace for David was a clean heart and a second chance to become a faithful King over Israel, leaving an eternal legacy. "*Create in me a clean heart, O God, and renew a right spirit within me,*" (Psalm 51:10). Amazing grace!

• God's amazing grace to Esther was "coming to the Kingdom for such a time as this," (Esther 4:14). God's amazing grace for His chosen people, the Jewish nation. Another picture of redemption! Amazing grace!

• God's amazing grace to Ruth was her second husband Boaz, her Redeemer Kinsman, and her place in the ancestry of Jesus, a beautiful picture for you and me of God's Son, Jesus, who would become our Redeemer Kinsman. Ruth 4:17 tells us of Ruth's son Obed, the father of Jesse, the father of David, the ancestor of Jesus Christ. Amazing grace!

• God's amazing grace for Paul was a blinding light—first the blinding light on the road to Damascus, which made him an apostle, then the light he became—a light to the Gentiles, and that is you and me. *"For the love of Christ controls us, having concluded this, that one died for all, therefore all died; and He died for all, that they who live should no longer live for themselves, but for Him who died and rose again on their behalf,"* (2 Corinthians 5:14). Amazing grace!

• God's amazing grace for the Samaritan woman was living water and quenched thirst. Jesus answered her saying, *"Everyone who drinks this water will be thirsty again, but whoever drinks the water I give him will never thirst. Indeed the water I give him will become in him a spring of water welling up to eternal life,"* (John 4: 14). Amazing grace!

• Amazing grace for Esther Burroughs was a Sunday School teacher in Canada who led me to understand John 3:16, and see that I was the "whosoever" that God loved so much. Amazing grace!

Who introduced you to God's amazing grace? I am sitting in my office writing this chapter...and feel overwhelmed that God's grace story includes a rag tag army, as Brennan Manning often says in his writings. I give thanks for the grace people that God has placed in my life. Ponder His grace upon grace in your story.

Chosen…by grace!
Blessed by grace!
Amazed by grace!

Healed by Grace

At age sixteen, she ran away from home. She wanted out! Leaving in the wee hours of morning, stealing her Dad's credit and debit cards, she purchased a bus ticket and headed for the West Coast. At no time on the long journey would she let herself think about home, especially mom's pancakes! She was on her own and free! That was all that mattered. It wasn't as if she didn't have everything she needed at home. Her parents were good and had prayed for the best for each of their children. It was her rebellion to be on her own, and be really free. You understand, don't you? Free…with Dad's credit and ATM cards…which she quickly maxed out. Making her way on the streets of her new city, she made friends quickly. It was easy, for her stolen money was still paying all the bills. She partied long into the night, night after night. Life was good! Love was free—well, at least a bed that came pretty cheap. No boundaries. No rules. On her own.

When the credit cards were reported and stopped, her life got a bit harder. The days were okay, but the night hours brought back the thoughts of her canopy bed…her bathroom…clean towels. How long had it been since she had had a hot shower and a hot meal? The memory became uppermost in her mind. A homeless shelter became her nighttime home, while lonely streets were her daytime residence.

Exhausted and hungry, she began to think about going back home. Desperate, she hitched a ride, heading toward her city, with a kind truck driver (God's grace in disguise) who convinced her to go home to her family.

Days later, dropping her at the edge of her hometown, he promised to pray for her safe return. Frightened, she hid behind a neighbor's bushes. She could see a light in the family room. While waiting for the light to go off, she just had to get a closer look. It was her daddy, sitting in his favorite chair, head bowed in prayer. Scared, she pulled back. She began to repeat over and over the thoughts she had been practicing: "I'm so sorry! I'm so sorry. Can you ever forgive me? Can I spend the night in my room and get a hot bath? Please, Daddy? Can I come home?"

The darkness of night turned into the early morning light. Encouraged when she saw her daddy was no longer in the chair, she made her way to the front door. There, to her surprise, she found this note: "Debbie! If you have made it this far, come on in! The door is unlocked. Welcome home!" Grace upon grace upon grace! Welcome words in any prodigal's ear.

Henry Nouwen's book, *The Return of the Prodigal*, is haunting in its truth and freeing in its grace. The biblical story is found in Luke 15:11-32. You know the story well. The tax collectors and sinners were coming to hear Jesus and the religious folk were grumbling, criticizing Jesus for receiving sinners and eating with them! How radical this Jesus was. Teaching them, Jesus told three stories about lost things: lost sheep, lost coins, and lost sons. Nouwen says:

> *One of the greatest challenges of the spiritual life is to receive forgiveness. There is something in us that keeps us clinging to our sins and prevents us from letting God erase our past and offer us a completely new beginning. We can't forgive what God has already forgiven. While God wants to restore me to full dignity of sonship, I keep insisting that I will settle for being a hired servant.*

Nouwen suggests in his book that each of us at times become the loving father, the prodigal, and the elder brother. We must keep searching to become like the loving father. Amazing grace! In the biblical account, the father calls both boys "son." The father treats the younger prodigal brother as if he had done nothing wrong, even throwing him an extravagant party. Grace upon grace!

The line in the Biblical narrative that grasps my heart is one that is spoken to the older brother. In Luke 15:31 the father says to the rule keeping elder brother, *"Son, you have always been with me, and all that is mine is yours."* Grace upon grace!

In other words, everything we need is found in the Father's house…through the Father's grace…at the Father's hand. Why do we search to fill our hearts with what the culture insists we need to be satisfied? Things! When the

Father says, "All that is mine is yours!" May the prodigal in each of us come home to our loving Heavenly Father and understand the heart of God for every prodigal, every elder brother, and every loving father—all invited to the party.

Forget Yesterday

My daughter Melody called me crying. Through her tears, she said: "I've just put Anna to bed and I've had the worst day. I've treated Anna awful! I'm a terrible mother." I listened. I prayed with her and then suggested she should apologize to Anna. The next day, she did apologize to her daughter. Three-year-old Anna responded: "What you do yet'terday, Mommy?" Her mother Melody recited all her failures (it's a woman thing to remember them). Anna said to her, "Forget yet'terday, Mommy!"

Jesus says the same to us: come home! All is forgiven! As the old hymn writer says: "Come home, come home. Ye who are weary, come home." Now that is amazing grace. Do you not weary of rule-keepers and rule-keeping in the faith? It does make one weary, doesn't it? What grace...to be able to forget yet'terday, and live in His grace...at the party!

A story is told of the late pastor, Dr. D. E. King. Upon graduating from seminary, he became pastor of a small church in Paducah, Kentucky. After moving into the parsonage, he decided to take a walk and become acquainted with his new community. It wasn't long before he spotted a slightly elderly woman across the street who was pushing a heavy grocery cart. He crossed the street, introduced himself, and offered to push her cart.

"What's your name?" he inquired.

"Folks 'round here call me Miss Stella."

"Well, Miss Stella, I'm the new pastor in town and I'd like you to be my guest at church tomorrow," he replied. Long pause.

"No one's ever asked me to that church before."

"Well, I want you to be my guest!"

When they arrived at Miss Stella's home, pastor King carried her groceries into the house and reminded her, as he walked away, that he would be counting on her to hear his first sermon in the morning.

When he arrived home from his walk, the phone was already ringing. One of his deacons called and said: "Now pastor, you are young and single and new in the community. What you don't know is this: Miss Stella is a woman of ill repute."

King answered, "I'm not concerned about her reputation and you need to be praying for her. I have invited her to come to church in the morning."

The word had gotten around town and Sunday morning, the church was packed. There was not an empty seat in the house. During the second hymn, the back door opened and in walked Miss Stella. Not finding a seat at the back, she just kept walking to the front. Dr. King looked down at the row of deacons and in his 6' 4" voice, invited the deacons to get up and give Miss Stella a seat. Instantly two deacons moved. Miss Stella sat down.

Dr. King ignored his prepared "first Sunday" sermon notes and told the story of the old rugged cross. At the invitation, Miss Stella stepped forward, tears rolling down her face. "No one has ever told me that story before!" she said to Dr. King. Miss Stella accepted God's love that morning and asked to speak to the congregation. She said "You all know the old Stella, but today, you're looking at the new Miss Stella." Revival broke out.

As the old hymn writer says: "Come home, come home. Ye who are weary, come home." Now that is amazing grace.

Dr. King delighted in telling people that Miss Stella went with him on his visitation days and she got him into places a preacher had never been before! She was his best visiting partner. When she passed away, the local newspaper reported these words: "Saint Stella died today."

I think the church is a hospital for recovering sinners, of whom I am chief. Everyone comes to Jesus in need of grace. What ever made us decide that prodigals and elder brothers can't stand side-by-side at the foot of the cross?

Parenting Teens with Grace

Every family has teen issues to get through with grace. Grace is the correct word. Someone(s) in your family is going to learn the grace factor. How come it is not an easy lesson? In fact, it is a lifelong lesson! Aren't you glad we get to see glimpses of it from time to time?

My lack of grace with my daughter kept showing up...always because of my expectations for her. How come my college students thought I was such a neat lady, but she didn't?

> "*Not that we are adequate in ourselves, but our adequacy is from God who also made us adequate as servants of a new covenant, not of the letter, but of the Spirit, for the letter kills, but the Spirit gives life.*" —2 Corinthians 4:7

That Scripture left me dead in the water! Day after day, year after year, living between grace and the law. The Holy Spirit began to show me in my Bible study time that I was far too concerned about what people thought of me. It was more about me being seen as pious than my desiring God's best for her. I wanted my daughter to have my walk with God.

Have you been there? Parents cannot give their faith to their children. It is a personal issue between God and child. I just spent so much time trying to be Holy Spirit Junior! Are you with me on this issue? Looking back is always clearer than looking from the middle. You know what I mean? But we can be helped through prayer.

My daughter and I wounded each other in the process. Because of grace and the Father's timing, healing began. I was in Europe on a choir tour with Bob and the Baptist

Festival Singers. On the trip, I read John Powell's little book, "Unconditional Love," and my eyes were opened. Calvary's love is all about grace amazing. All the time my precious daughter and I were struggling, God had given her an adopted mother who was loving her just for herself. I could not wait to get home from that trip and ask my daughter's forgiveness. She picked me up at the airport, hands full of flowers and love in her heart. I could see it in her eyes. My heart raced! I had memorized how I would ask for her forgiveness. I don't remember how Bob got home, Melody and I just drove off together. On that hot Birmingham, Alabama day, we parked the car outside a Christmas Shop in English Village, and talked.

I said, "Let me go first! I have to tell you something before I burst."

She said, "No! Let me go first! I've learned so much about myself while you were gone."

I said, "Please! Let me go first!"

So we both talked at once. She talked about the college tests she had just taken and how it showed her aptitudes and how the counselor had helped her understand herself in light of her upbringing. I told her how John Powell's book had broken my heart in showing me unconditional love. (She had pointed out to me several times my lack of it! UGH!) We wept, each asking for forgiveness and a new beginning, and a fresh start. Dear reader, I've been graced over and over with fresh starts. I trust you have, too! I pray we will learn to stand in His grace as many times as necessary, till we get it! I pray we get so good at grace living that our family notices, our neighbors notice, and the Father is glorified!

Healed by grace!
Blessed by grace!
Amazed by grace!

Stunned by Grace

I have learned so much through other writers, and one of my favorites is the late Mike Yaconelli. His book *Dangerous Wonder* is all about joy and freedom in the faith. In chapter 8, Mike retells the Biblical parable of the wealthy man preparing a lavish banquet who ends up inviting those in the highways and hedges, the misfits of life. He says there is no room in the church for arrogance because none of us belong there! Mike tells the following story about himself.

> *For a number of years, my wife and I volunteered with a Young Life Club in our town. One year, a young man in our club was obviously having a difficult year. He was not doing well in school, was in and out of juvenile hall, and my wife and I struck up a friendship with him. His home was a mess. His Dad was an alcoholic who emotionally and physically abused the entire family. For six months, we spent a lot of time*

with this young man while his Dad went through detox.

We would have forgotten the entire experience if it weren't for some remodeling we did on our house. We decided to redo the tile in our kitchen, and, because we live in a small town, we ordered the tile from the "big city" sixty miles away. When our special order arrived, the tile company told us they didn't have enough personnel to lay the tile for three weeks, but we could get the job done immediately if we used someone local. We had no problem with a local person, until they gave us his name.

"Absolutely not!" I yelled into the phone. "That man is an alcoholic, knocks his family around and I don't trust him!" He was the father of the young man we had helped. Startled, the person on the phone promised to get someone else. Two days later, the tile company called back with bad news. Except for this one person, everyone in town was booked up. We wanted the tile done soon, so I reluctantly agreed to hire the man. I told my wife, "I am going to watch him like a hawk. He is not going to cheat me." I demanded a written estimate, and I got one for $350 for three days work. Each day he was laying tile, I would check on his work.

On the third day it looked like he would finish on time. I walked by and said, "When you're done, come by my office and I'll write you a check." "Oh," he said, "I need to talk to you about the money. I'll talk to you when I'm done."

I stormed out to my office (which is in my garage next to my wife's office) and angrily reported to my wife. "I knew it. I knew he was going to try to cheat us out of some money. Well, I have a signed contract, and I am not going to pay him one more dime than we agreed."

I ranted and raved for another few minutes and then bragged to my wife: "Leave the door between our offices open so you can see how I handle this guy. I will not pay him one dime more that we agreed to."

At 5 P.M., the tile layer walked into my office and sat down directly across from my desk, and began writing out a bill. I was ready for him and glanced at my wife with the look of testosterone on my face. He started to hand me the bill, but then paused for a moment and said: "A couple of years ago, I was drinking too much. I am an alcoholic and was at a very low point in my life. I almost lost my family because of my drinking. I mistreated my wife and my children, especially my oldest son. But you and your wife spent a lot of time with him at that critical moment in his life when he could have gone either way. Shortly after that time, I went to AA, and I've been sober ever since. Because of you and your wife, I still *have a relationship with my son. I've never been able to thank you, but I'm thanking you now." He handed me his bill for $350. "Paid in full" was written across the page. We shook hands and he walked out. Humiliated, I slumped down in my chair, speechless. This alcoholic, abusing, untrustworthy man had just shown this arrogant, self-righteous snob the meaning of grace. The grace of God levels us all. All of us are broken...all of us are flawed...all of us are undeserving. There's no room in the church for pride, a judgmental attitude, or arrogance. All of us have had our debt "paid in full."*

Stunned by grace!
Blessed by grace!
Amazed by grace!

Covered by Grace

I know firsthand of the measureless overflowing of the fountain of the grace of God. Early December 1955, I was at Mars Hill College, walking up the hill to Huffman Dorm. The campus sound system began playing familiar Christmas songs. I did all right with "Frosty, the Snowman" but when "I'll Be Home for Christmas" began, the tears started. Bob was with me and did not know what to say or do. Not much one can do with homesickness...except be sick. I know! I had it often.

I had come to Mars Hill College with $350 in my pocket. I was privileged to work my way through college. Tuition, room and board for a year was $600 in 1955! I came on faith that God would provide work so I could pay the bill. He did. When I left my home in Edmonton, Alberta, Canada, my preacher daddy could not afford to bring me home for Christmas. My head knew that, but my heart was longing for a Canadian White Christmas.

With several kind invitations in hand to go home with friends, and with exams almost completed, I was given a final assignment by some friends. It would be my responsibility to get my across-the-hall and good friend, Paddy Wall, to the cafeteria on Saturday morning for her surprise birthday party! I remember being shaken awake by Paddy the next morning telling me to get up and get to her party! We laughed as I got dressed and off we went to the cafeteria. I'm sure I told Paddy to act surprised.

Bringing my friend into the cafeteria, I was in for the surprise of my life! A huge banner hung over the balcony of the cafeteria with these words: Merry Christmas, Esther Milligan! The students had collected money to send me home for Christmas, by train, to Canada. Tears flowed. They gave me enough money to call home—long distance—to tell my parents. Remember, in 1955, there were no cell phones, or dorm room phones! We just had the hall phone booth. My friends gathered outside the booth and I dropped the coins in the phone. When I heard my Dad's voice. I began to cry as I told him, "I'm coming home for Christmas!"

He said, "You can't do that, Esther!"

I said, "Yes I can! The students are sending me home by train." I was so excited I did not even tell him when I would arrive! I've never ever gotten over that gift of grace.

After that Christmas with my family, I was riding the train back to Asheville, NC, when a snow slide derailed the train in Winnipeg, Manitoba. All the passengers were put off the train and placed in one of the Canadian Pacific Railroad Hotels. We were assigned rooms and I had about five dollars to my name! I did not eat the next meal, for I had no idea how much the room would cost. I vividly remember a rather loud wedding party at the end of my hall, celebrating and dancing after the ceremony. Frightened, I climbed up on the dresser and locked the overhead window, which was the room's only ventilation, while trying to keep myself safe. I fell asleep in fear, Bible open to the Psalms, claiming God's protection from those party people. How I wish that I'd known then that Jesus loved parties. I'd have joined the party, helped myself to the food and probably slept better!

The next morning, the passengers were given free breakfast and charged nothing for the room. What a relief! We were then placed on a special express train, through Chicago and on into Asheville, NC. We arrived at exactly the time I had been scheduled to arrive! On the train platform stood Bob Burroughs and Dr. Emmett Sams, my favorite professor, waiting for me.

Grace upon grace every step of the way, even the grace I did not recognize: a wedding party—full of joy and God's grace covering on a shy college student. I wasted a lot of time living by the Law, hiding under the Word instead of celebrating the Truth, while everyone else was having a great time dancing at the party. I'm getting it though. A decade of college students deeply engraved my heart with their grace and acceptance. An incredible staff at the Home Mission Board taught me to serve in grace. My own children graced me over and over by telling me when I wasn't grace. My grandchildren are teaching me grace.

The secret to living in grace—stand in it! Romans 5:2 teaches us, *"Therefore, having been justified by faith, we have peace with God through our Lord Jesus Christ, through whom we have access by faith into this grace in which we stand, and rejoice in hope of the Glory of God."*

I know the Grace Giver!
I cherish the grace given!
I'm blessed to stand in grace!

Blessed by Grace

On the Sunday morning of my dad's 98th birthday celebration weekend, he was asked to dedicate two of his great-grandchildren…a boy and a girl. They stood in front of the church as my dad preached—yes, preached a message to the parents of his great-grandchildren. He gave a clear challenge to raise these children by the Word of God and to make sure they were in the house of God. His energy level was so high that he was on his tiptoes. He prayed and blessed them. It was, indeed, a holy moment...seeing four generations praying together.

After church, we all gathered at our adopted mother's home on Lake Martin, the home of Mrs. Jackie Lee. Photos were taken of each of the four-generation families. It was a special day indeed for all of us. Since Dad had 15 of his great-grandchildren gathered that weekend, I asked him if he would pray a blessing over all of them. It was quite a feat to gather them together, because they ranged in age from 18 months to 15 years.

We gathered all the great-grands around him and he prayed a special blessing over them. Yes, we video-recorded this legacy moment. We plan to add his prayer blessing to a CD that contains a few of the handwritten prayers in his book, blessing generations to come, allowing them to see a legacy of 98 years of Godly living. What better grace can we give the generations to come than blessing of prayer? It is our job! It is our joy! My heart's passion is to reach this generation with the challenge to pass the baton of a spiritual legacy, to be a blessing even to generations yet to be born.

Let this be your passion too. Don't drop the baton! Pass on spiritual legacies to the next generation! I want to end this book with a prayer from King David, one that I hope will be your prayer as well:

"And now, great God, this word that You have spoken to me and my family, guarantee it permanently! Do exactly what you have promised! Then your reputation will flourish always as people explain, 'The GOD-of-the-Angel-Armies is God over Israel!' And the house of your servant David will remain sure and solid in your watchful presence. For you, GOD-of-the-Angel-Armies, Israel's God, told me plainly, 'I will build you a house.' That's how I was able to find courage to pray this prayer to you. And now, Master God, being the God You are, speaking sure words as You do, and having just said this wonderful thing to me, please, just one more thing: Bless my family; keep Your eye on them always. You've already as much as said that you would, Master GOD! Oh, may your blessing be on my family permanently!"

—2 Samuel 7:25–29 (*The Message*)

Legacies
～ OF GRACE

- Bless your children every day, eight times a day, by touch, smiles, words, notes, laughter, touches, encouragement, and prayers.

- Bless God by opening the Bible as you sit around the kitchen table/dining table.

- Grace a child by giving them freedom from chores for a day.

- Set family goals for the next six months.

- Grace each of your children with individual time with Mom or Dad regularly.

- Grace your family by keeping in touch as parents. Have parent's couch time—ten minutes to debrief the day together.

- Have a Sunday night tradition of hot dogs, grilled cheese sandwiches, pizza, whatever you all like!

- Have a "No TV Week."

- Have an "At-Home Weekend" when all family members will be at home.

- Have an all hands-on-deck family project weekend.

- Bless your children every chance you get.